Geulah
b'rachamim

Sixty daily lessons to help a Jew
yearn for redemption

THIRTYSIX.ORG

Pinchas Winston

First Printing: June 2008
Second Printing: July 2008

Geulah b'Rachamim

60 daily lessons to help a Jew yearn for redemption

ISBN 978-0-9784025-4-9

Published and Distributed by:

Thirtysix.org
POB 292
Telzstone, Kiryat Yearim,
Israel   90838

Printed at:

Old City Press
30 Beit HaDafus
Jerusalem, Israel
oldcitypress@netvision.net.il

To access the *Geulah b'Rachamim* site, and the PowerPoint Presentation, go to **www.thirtysix.org**.

We are pleased to have this opportunity to be a part of this important project on behalf of *Klal Yisroel*. May our involvement be a merit for

Binyamin Boruch ben Avrohom, z"l
(Bernard Ziegler)

and

Chaya bas Beryl Dov, z"l
(Harriet Ziegler)

their children
Alan and Sophia Ziegler

On a recent speaking trip, I stopped over in Monsey to make a presentation of this material, not knowing, at the time, the real purpose of my stop there.

As it turned out, the host was sufficiently affected by the material to ask me, *"What are you doing about getting this out there? More Jews have to know about all of this, and quick!"* I told him, *"That is why I am here! To enlist people like yourself to help spread the message before it becomes too late!"*

After watching the PowerPoint presentation, we ended by brainstorming that night for about an hour, and then for another hour the next morning on the way to the airport. Being the marketing genius that he is, his suggestions came fast and furious, and were extremely helpful.

One major result: *"Geulah b'Rachamim"*.

As always, I am extremely grateful to *Hashem Yisborach* for everything I have and am able to do. However, I can now add to that list the opportunity to have met Aharon Levi (Alan) Proctor that night, who has been a tremendous source of ideas, advice, and encouragement, all the way through this project.

Also, as always, I thank my wife, Ahava, and our children, and our parents, Jack and Betty Winston, and Avrom and Roslyn Neumark, for their tremendous ongoing love and support.

Thank you to Rabbi Noach Weinberg, *shlita*, as always. May this book only add to his countless merits, and contribute to his well-being.

Thank you to all the *rabbanim* who have taught me over the years, especially Rabbi Mordechai Friedlander, *shlita*, who once again has taken time from his very hectic schedule to review my work. The Rav has said that "... just like with respect to the previous books, this is a beautiful, well-sourced work that clearly shows the importance of appreciating the gift of *Eretz Yisroel*, and how a Jew must make great effort to anticipate the redemption."

Thank you to all of my supporters, material and spiritual, who believe in what I teach, and have once again made this project possible.

Last, but certainly not least, I would like to show a tremendous amount of appreciation to a *rebi* I have never met. Indeed, he left this world 34 years before I was even born. However, without doubt, he has had one of the most profound impacts on my life, thinking, and writings: Rabbi Shlomo Eliyashiv, *zt"l* (1841-1925), the grandfather of present-day *Gadol HaDor*, Rabbi Yosef Shalom Eliyashiv, *shlita*.

Otherwise known as the "*Ba'al HaLeshem*," after the name of his *seforim*, "*Leshem Shevo v'Achlamah*" (these are the names of the three stones in the third row of breastplate worn by the *Kohen Gadol*; *Shemos* 27:19), he remains one of the greatest Kabbalists in recent times. However, until a friend of mine showed up one day at my front door with a copy of the *"Sha'arei Leshem"*, saying, *"Here, we have to learn this sefer!"* I had never heard of the *Leshem* at all.

Nevertheless, once I began learning his *seforim*, I could not stop. There is no way to adequately describe the depth of his thinking, or his incredible ability to synthesize concepts, and present them in a clear and understandable manner. This was made possible by his awesome mastery over every aspect of Torah, and on many occasions, water welled up in my eyes from the beauty of Torah that was revealed through his pen.

One unique aspect of the *Leshem's* teachings is the depth to which he deals with topics such as, *Yemos HaMoshiach*, *Techiyas HaMeisim*, and *Olam HaBah*. In fact, though it had never been my intention to be involved with such controversial matters, I was so overwhelmed by what I was discovering that I felt compelled to share knowledge that was becoming increasingly more crucial with each passing day. *Geulah b'Rachamim* is only the most current example of such an effort.

Recently, articles have appeared discussing the life and greatness of the *Leshem*. Not only this, but more of his *sefarim* have been re-printed, and made available to the general public, making sure that his light can continue to guide us through the darkness of exile, and so that his merit can help us to bring the final redemption, mercifully.

Pinchas Winston
Telzstone, Iyar 5768

live up to its spiritual potential? Especially now, as world leaders attempt to divide the holy city of God.

Temple times. However, with the return of the temple service, both the *Kohanim* and the *Levi'im* will return to the roles they once played on behalf of the entire Jewish nation.

just wait to see what happens? When it comes to Jewish history, that is rarely a good idea.

hopeless. That was not incidental, but part of the redemption process, and the sooner we learn its lesson, the less we have to go through it.

it is not always a matter of simply opening your eyes. Many people see things, but they don't know what they are looking at, or why they need to respond to it, as Pinchas did in the Torah.

Using This Book

Geulah b'Rachamim is not a book that is meant to be read once or twice and then put aside. Rather, it is meant to be a guide to help people navigate the rarely discussed path to redemption, and to shed light on some of the more confusing events of the day.

The 60 lessons contain many concepts that must be reviewed on an constant basis, in order to gain a deeper appreciation of their meaning, and to integrate their messages. Each lesson is brief, and to the point, but all of them discuss ideas of tremendous significance, not just for preparing for the Final Redemption, but for becoming a more complete Torah Jew. Therefore, the reader should take time to contemplate both the stated and implied meaning of each lesson.

Though it may not always be obvious, the 60 lessons follow a specific order. In a sense, they represent a single stream of consciousness, and therefore, it is important to follow the order of the book, at least the first time through.

The entire book is designed to be completed six times within the course of one year. There is chart at the end of the book that shows the six cycles, since the date of the first cycle alone is provided on the actual daily lesson.

Why 60 lessons? This number was chosen because of its Kabbalistic significance and relationship to the concept of redemption. For, being a number that embodies the major part of 100, which represents spiritual perfection, 60 alludes to abundance and completion (*Maharal, Aggados* 2).

Furthermore, in the *Aleph-Bais*, the number 60 is represented by the letter *Samech*. As such, it is associated with the word "*samach*", which means "support", alluding to the assistance that man requires from God just to survive, let alone to be redeemed from exile.

Lesson 35, which discusses Tisha B'Av, was written to be learned on Tisha B'Av itself. As a result, the first lesson of the book begins on the fourth of Tammuz, but obviously, the reader can follow whatever schedule works best for him.

The hope is that the 60 lessons, *b'ezras Hashem*, will become the basis of a national movement that will help refocus the Jewish people back on their ultimate national goal of redemption. Based upon the sources found in the upcoming lessons, and examples from our long history, doing so can only result in a more favorable *Hashgochah Pratis*, and a redemption that comes more peacefully than it seems to be approaching at this time, *R"L*.

---

[1] The *sefirah Yesod*, which corresponds to the sixth millennium, the one in which redemption is destined to occur (*Hakdamos v'Sha'arim*, p. 172), is represented by the number six. The number 60, which corresponds to the *sefirah* of *Tifferes*, which is intimately connected to *Yesod* and redemption (just as Ya'akov Avinu was close to Yosef HaTzaddik, the ancestor of Moshiach Ben Yosef) is merely a multiple of this (*Zohar* 2:9b).

On a personal note, the reason for this project is a concern for the future of the Jewish people. Comparatively-peaking, our generation has been living through a relatively pleasant period of history, *thank God*. However, it is not the first time, and if history has anything to teach us, it is how quickly the good times can become difficult and painful ones for the Jewish nation.

No one wants to hear that. We have become so over-sensitive to criticism that even the slightest hint of negativity, these days, can send readers in the opposite direction. Pointing out the negative potential of current events, even if backed up by Torah sources and past experience, is often seen as unwarranted pessimism, and rejected out-of-hand.[2]

However, think of it like a doctor who, after examining a patient, discovers something in the patient's body that is dangerous and in need of serious treatment. It's never easy to tell a patient unsettling news. However, what choice does the doctor have? If he downplays the seriousness of the situation, the patient will be lax and negligent in taking his life-saving treatment.

The premise of this book is that the Jewish people today are in a spiritually "unhealthy" situation that requires treatment, *while the patient is still healthy enough to do something about it*. We may, as a people, feel good about ourselves, having accomplished so much over the last few decades. However, if our past has anything at all to teach

---

[2] This is not something new. Apparently, even the prophets of olden days were ignored by many, in spite of the fact that their messages came directly from God. If so, then what can we expect today when we have only tradition, *seforim*, and past experience to guide us through difficult times?

us, it is to ask ourselves, *"Are we doing everything right as far as Heaven is concerned?"*

Recent historical trends regarding the Jewish people, together with those from the past, seem to say, *"Not necessarily."* In spite of all the good we have accomplished over the years and all around the world, something still seems to be missing, after thousands of years of history, and so close to the end.

This is a campaign to help Jews appreciate the need to become more *geulah*-oriented, and the consequences of not doing so. It is not a message that we can afford to dilute, nor is it one that we can allow to be softened by the outspoken voices of political correctness. Doing so may feel good today, but it will only make matters worst tomorrow. Seemingly, it always has.

It was decided to publish the book before it was fully dedicated. Therefore, anyone who would like to make a (U.S. tax deductible) dedication in the next printing of the book can write to:

geulahbrachamim@mac.com

or

Thirtysix.org
POB 292
Telzstone, Kiryat Yearim
Israel   90838
Fax: 02-533-2811

I believe with perfect faith in the coming of *Moshiach*, and even though he may tarry, I will wait for him, for any day he can come. (Principle #12, *The Thirteen Principles of Faith*)

It is fundamental to Torah belief that there will be a final redemption of the Jewish people. At some point in time, someone from the dynasty of Dovid *HaMelech* will eventually herald the end of history as we know it, the return of the Jewish people from the lands of their exile to the Land of Israel, and the establishment of a Torah government on the land. It is not a question of *if*, but of *when*, and of *how*.

So central is this belief to a Torah Jew, that it is associated with the first of the Ten Commandments:

The *Sefer Mitzvos HaKatan* wrote in his explanation of the Positive *Mitzvah* of, "*I am God, your God, Who took you out of Egypt,*" that it means one must know that He Who created Heaven and Earth alone controls above and below. However, to this he added, "This is the basis for what the rabbis teach: At the time of a person's judgment after death, they ask him, 'Did you anticipate redemption?' (*Shabbos* 31a). Where is this *mitzvah* written? Actually, it comes from here, for, just as, '*I am God, your God, Who took you out of Egypt*' means that we are expected to believe that God redeemed us from Egypt, it also means: Just as I want you to believe that I took you out [from Egypt], I also want you to believe that I, God your God, will gather you in and redeem you in mercy a second time." (*Ohr Yechezkel, Emunas HaGeulah*, 1960; p. 287)

However, what a Jew has to know is that there are two possible ways in which the Final Redemption can come, peacefully, or after a great war, which is referred to by the prophets of *Tanach* as, the War of Gog and Magog:

> After *Moshiach* comes, a major war will be instigated against Israel, as mentioned in the Holy *Zohar* (*Shemos* 7b); see this at length until page 10. It is also in *Parashas Vayaira* (119a) and *Parashas Toldos* (139). This is the War of Gog and Magog spoken about in *Yechezkel* (Ch. 38; 39), and *Zechariah* (Ch. 14), as well as in *Midrash Tehillim* (*Mizmor* 118:9): Three times in the future Gog and Magog will war with Israel and go up against Jerusalem; they will assemble and anger the nations to go up to Jerusalem with him, as it explains there. Also see *Vayikra Rabbah* (27:11), and many other places. (*Sha'arei Leshem*, p. 491)

Based upon the descriptions of this war in the books of the prophets, it is a war to be avoided at all costs. Avoiding it, according to the Talmud, is a function of the actions of the Jewish people at the time:

Sanhedrin 98a.

Rav said, "All the dates of redemption have already passed, and now it depends upon repentance and good deeds." Shmuel said, "It is enough that the mourner remains in mourning!" This is like an earlier disagreement: Rebi Eliezer said, "If Israel will repent then they will be redeemed, and if they will not, then they will not." Rebi Yehoshua said to him, "If they do not repent they will not be redeemed?! Rather, The Holy One, Blessed is He, will cause a king to arise who will make decrees as difficult as Haman's, and Israel will repent and return to the right path." (*Sanhedrin* 97b)

We know who Haman was, the second-in-command of Persia during the time of the Purim miracle. We recall each year the decrees of destruction he made against the Jewish people, and what would have resulted had Heaven not interceded on our behalf. We can read for ourselves how difficult life became for the Jewish people, until God finally ended his reign of tyranny. And, we can assume that we do not want another one to arise in order to remind us of what we would should be focusing on in advance of *Moshiach's* arrival.

Therefore, the mission is to empower all Jews to help bring the Final Redemption more safely. The main means of accomplishing this goal is the creation of a booklet containing 60 short, yet powerful, daily study lessons, which will progressively focus people on the main goals of the Jewish People, and of history in general.

Without doubt, as more Jews join the program and increase their commitment to the idea of redemption, the more mercy Heaven will show to *Tzion*. With history heading down a path that does not forebode well for the Jewish people, we are obligated to do whatever we can to mitigate any negative events that might be heading our way, *Chas v'Shalom*.

In the past, the passive approach to redemption has never served us well. There is no reason to assume that it will now. And, as this book will make clear, the main difference between a peaceful redemption and one that has been described in frightening detail in the Book of the Prophets, may simply be a change of heart.

Tammuz 4

DAY ONE:
Learn to Yearn

Dovid *HaMelech* wrote:

> *You will arise and show Tzion mercy, for the time to favor her, for the appointed time will have come. For your servants have cherished her stones and favor her dust.* (*Tehillim* 102:14-15)

Dovid *HaMelech* was writing about the Final Redemption, indicating that its time will have come when the Jewish people cherish *Eretz Yisroel*, even her stones and dust. This is very important to know if we want to usher in *Yemos HaMoshiach* peacefully.

The Talmud, at the end of *Kesuvos* speaks about rabbis of the Second Temple period, and the seemingly menial things they did to show their love of *Eretz Yisroel*. One fixed the potholes in the road, one literally rolled in the dust (*Kesuvos* 112a), etc., whatever they could do to show Hashem their appreciation for living on the land.

Given that we are in exile to this very day because the generation of the Spies rejected *Eretz Yisroel*, it is not hard to understand the intense desire of the rabbis of the Talmud to show appreciation for the gift of the land. They understood the connection between God's mercy on Tzion and our attachment to the concept of redemption and *Eretz Yisroel*.

This is certainly one of the main tests of this generation, which is enjoying unprecedented success amongst the nations of the world. People tend to cherish and yearn most for the place in which they feel the most at home. After having been raised in the Western world, it is difficult for many Jews to relate to living in *Eretz Yisroel*.

In the end, it is all a question of priorities, and of understanding and relating to the ultimate goals of the Jewish nation. For example, the Torah commands us to be a holy nation, and we do that best in *Eretz Yisroel*. While scattered amongst the nations, we can't properly serve Hashem as a people, especially without a temple. That affects the quality of our spiritual lives now, and our portion in the World-to-Come later.

Think about something that you yearn for, and ask yourself why. See how yearning for it affects your life, and what you are prepared to do to acquire it. Then, ask yourself why you don't feel the same way about redemption, and *Eretz Yisroel*. Then, consider what you can do to change all of that.

Remember, a merciful redemption can occur without making a single change in location or lifestyle. It just takes a change of heart.

Tammuz 5

DAY TWO:
Willing To Go?

Only one-fifth of the Jewish population in Egypt at the time, actually left with Moshe *Rabbeinu*. As *Rashi* explains, four-fifths died in the Plague of Darkness, as Rabbi Yechezkel Levenstein reiterates:

> The exodus from Egypt liberated only one out of five Jews—and some say one out of every 50—because all those who were bound to Egypt and did not want to depart died in the three days of darkness and were not privileged to leave. That is, only those who desired redemption with all their hearts were redeemed. (*Ohr Yechezkel, Emunas HaGeulah*, p. 288)

However, Rabbi Levenstein adds:

> The Final Redemption, likewise, depends upon our yearning. (Ibid.)

The truth is, Rabbi Levenstein is simply repeating what the Talmud itself teaches:

> It was taught: Rebi Simai said, "It says, '*I will take you to Me as a people*' (*Shemos* 6:7), and it says, '*And I will bring you to the land*' (Ibid. 8). Just as the coming to the land [of Israel]

was with two of the 60 myriads,[1] so too was the leaving of Egypt with two of the 60 myriads." Rava said, "It will be likewise in *Yemos HaMoshiach*, as it says, '*She will dwell there as in the days of her youth, and as on the day of her ascent from Egypt*' (Hoshea 2:17)." (*Sanhedrin* 111a)

This means that, 3,000,000 Jews left Egypt for freedom; 12,000,000 Jews perished in the Plague of Darkness, and all because they had no desire to leave exile!

It also means that, just as in the time of the redemption from Egypt, at the end of history, when *Moshiach* leads the Final Redemption, four-fifths of the Jewish population will not heed the call. They won't want to leave exile, and may suffer the consequences for their decision. The Jews of Egypt had intended to stay behind and prosper, but instead, they perished in the ninth plague and never witnessed the redemption.

A Jew has to ask himself, "If *Moshiach* came today and rallied the Jews to return home, would I be willing to go? Would I be ready to go? Would I be happy to go? Would I be part of the one-fifth to leave, if that is all that survives, *God forbid*?"

Answering these questions will allow a person to see what he needs to do to ready himself for redemption. The answer to each question, eventually, has to be yes. If it is not, you have to understand why, and what it would take to change your mind and your heart.

Dedicated Anonymously

---

[1] One myriad is equal to 10,000 people, so 60 myriads would equal 600,000 people.

שורשים השקעות
תפארת ישראל 3 ירושלים
טל. 02-6289729

שורשים
מסרף 4247115 LIP-309-4S
מספר עסק 0316174
שעה 12:57 תאריך 12/01/09
כרטיס אמריקן אקספרס
מס' 372835091113000
בתוקף עד סוף 04/09
---- שובר : 61001004 ----

אישור 5654090 - ת - חברה

חירב בש"ח
SALE
אופן ביצוע: רגיל
סוג האשראי: רגיל

=========
NIS 59.00
=========

HAVE A NICE DAY

מרכול

חשבונית מס'

SALE

~~~~~~~~~~~~~~
NIS 59.00
~~~~~~~~~~~~~~

HAVE A NICE DAY

Tammuz 6

DAY THREE:
What's Driving You?

An interesting piece of information that is especially relevant to our generation comes from the *Arizal*, who taught:

> In the future, Moshe himself will reincarnate and return in the last generation, as it says, "*you will die with your fathers and rise up*" (*Devarim* 31:16). In fact, in the final generation, the *Dor HaMidbar* will also reincarnate with the *Erev Rav* ... Thus, the Generation of the Desert along with the *Erev Rav* will reincarnate in the final generation, "*like in the days of leaving Egypt*" (*Michah* 7:15). (*Sha'ar HaGilgulim*, Ch. 20)

Difficult as this may be to believe, the *Arizal* revealed that the souls of the Jewish people at the end of history will be the same souls of the Jewish people from the beginning of our history. One of the main reasons for this will be *tikun*, that is, rectification of the sin that they committed.

We already saw how four-fifths of the Jewish population in Egypt died in the Plague of Darkness for not wanting to leave Egypt. However, from the one-fifth that did leave, millions died over the course of 39 years, for not wanting to go into *Eretz Yisroel*, and it is those souls that return at the end of history to make amends for that tragic sin.

It is important to recall that the Spies who spoke badly about *Eretz Yisroel* had been leaders of the people. The people themselves had experienced the exodus from Egypt, the splitting of the sea, and the giving of Torah by God Himself. They were, therefore, on a very high spiritual level, and could only have heeded the Spies' advice, if doing so, had appeared as a *mitzvah* in their eyes. That is why they were shocked by God's reaction, and tried immediately to ascend to *Eretz Yisroel* as a result.

Before anyone belittles *Eretz Yisroel* and the idea of *aliyah*, he has to ask himself, "Where does that urge come from?" He or she has to wonder, "Am I perpetuating the sin of the Spies? Am I here to rectify that sin, and failing to do so? Should I feel less confident about my negative attitude towards the land of my fathers?"

We may not be able to answer the questions with certainty. However, it would be foolish to downplay the possibility, that our being present at this late stage, is primarily to rectify at the end of our history what went wrong at the beginning of our history. It's our soul that drives us. In a generation that has the possibility of living in *Eretz Yisroel* as well as in the Diaspora, it helps to know which one.

Tammuz 7

DAY FOUR:
See Divine Providence

Yosef said to his brothers, "I am Yosef, is my father still alive?"
But his brothers weren't able to answer him because they
were in shock. (Bereishis 45:3)

One of the most famous stories in the Torah is that of
Yosef and his brothers, the climax being when Yosef finally
revealed his identity to them, to their utter shock and
amazement. After being separated for 22 years, the brothers
discovered, much to their consternation, just how wrong
they had been about Yosef and his dreams.

So powerful was Yosef's revelation and the brother's
reaction that the rabbis use it as an metaphor of what it will
be like for every Jew on the final day of judgment. All God
will have to say is, "I am God", and many will fall back in
shock when they realize how many times throughout the
course of their lives God tried to help them do the right
thing, and they didn't pay attention.

The Torah says that Yosef only revealed himself to his
brothers because he saw that Yehudah was prepared to go
to war against all of Egypt, in order to save Binyomin. Apparently, Yosef had wanted to continue concealing his
identity, but could not, in order to avert a major catastrophe.

The question is, why? At what point would he have wanted to end the charade and save his brothers, and his father, any further anguish? What was left to be gained at that point by keeping his true identity a secret?

Rethinking the entire story, it is clear that Yosef was trying to encourage the brothers to come to the conclusion on their own, that it was Yosef who stood before them as viceroy of Egypt. He was trying to help them to learn to see past the external barriers, and to see the inner essence of who he was. He wanted them to conclude on their own, "You must be Yosef!"

Who else could have known what kind of wood was used to make their cribs? Who else would inquire so much about their family, and about their father's welfare? The viceroy of Egypt? Hardly. A long-lost family member, who had dreams of being king one day? Hard to believe, but far more likely.

The Midrash says:

All that happened to Yosef will happen to Tzion. (*Tanchuma, Vayaishev* 10)

This means that the Jewish people are likely to misread history at the end of days, finding it difficult to believe that ancient prophecies are coming true before their very eyes. Until, that is, history itself makes it impossible to believe otherwise.

The question to ask is, "When that happens, will I be shocked, or pleasantly surprised?" Upon what will it depend? How clearly you can see the hand of God in all that is taking place; whether or not you can take seriously the Divine Providence directing history.

The person who can say, "You are God!" today will be able to say it on the Day of Judgment as well. For, that is someone who can see the hand of God in all that happens, and how what is taking place is actually the fulfillment of the ultimate plan for Creation.

In honor of
Max (Chayim) ben Yitzhak Mizrahi
Yitzhak ben Jacob Mizrahi
Mourad Ezra Douek

In memory of
Aron ben Faivel Weisenfeld

Mr. & Mrs. Gerald Mizrahi

Tammuz 8

DAY FIVE:
Know Your History

As with many important things in life, context counts for a lot when it comes to appreciating current events. Out of context, a comment can be offensive; in context, it can be completely appropriate and understandable. How many misunderstandings throughout history have occurred because something was taken out of context?

This is true, not just about statements people make, but about life in general. Our lives need context too, meaning that we need to appreciate the historical backdrop against which we live out our lives, especially when it comes to the more dramatic events. Without context, we can completely overlook the meaning of an event, and miss the opportunity of a moment.

Hence, the Torah tells us:

Remember the days of old, understand the many generations that have passed. Ask your father, and he will tell you; your elders, and they will say it to you. (Devarim 32:7)

Sometimes, it is not enough to only know the past, but one must know the future as well, when possible. Therefore, the Torah is filled with prophecies about the future, and God gave the Jewish people the Book of the Prophets, which begins where the Torah ended. The present always looks different in light of the future.

Thus, we find that Ya'akov *Avinu*, on his deathbed, tried to reveal to his sons what would happen at the End-of-Days. And, this was even though he knew that they probably wouldn't occur until long after they were gone from this world.

Nevertheless, such information would have helped the Jewish people to remain focused on the long term goals of the nation, while in the depths of exile. Without such clarity, wide-scale assimilation and intermarriage were likely, as history has now proven. Without such clarity, even religious Jews stop yearning for redemption, and that does not invoke Divine mercy, just the opposite.

It is amazing how different current history looks once a Jew starts learning *Tanach* on a regular basis. By getting in touch with our past, and by being aware of our future, a shift in the way we perceive life and history in general occurs. Then we become better able to appreciate the events of our lives, and better prepared for what may be coming up. And that *does* invoke Divine mercy.

Dedicated by Mr. & Mrs. Jonathan Straight

Tammuz 9

DAY SIX:
Historical Deadlines

"Hey, Avi, what's the rush?"
"I have to get to minyan!"
"Relax, there are at least four more after this one."
"I can't wait. If I'm late for work one more time, I'll lose my job!"
"Oh, in that case, you better hurry up!"

It is amazing how certain pieces of information can change everything. What can seem like an endless amount of time to accomplish something can quickly become insufficient time, once a deadline is realized.

"Weren't you there at the meeting when the boss announced the deadline?"
"No, I skipped that meeting! I had no idea that we have to complete everything in two weeks!"
"Well, you better put in a lot of overtime and work double time, or else you'll lose your job!"
"I can't believe this! And I was about to take some time off with my family!"

The same is true about Jewish history: it has deadlines as well. Indeed, just finding out about them can change one's entire perspective on life, especially when we live so late in history. It reveals the true context of our lives.

For example, the Talmud states that history, as we know it, is only meant to last 6,000 years (*Sanhedrin* 97a). This would mean that, as of the writing of this book, there are only 232 years left until Year 6000, by which time, *Moshiach* will have already come and rectified the world. There will be no need for *Moshiach* after the year 6000.

Furthermore, explains the Vilna Gaon, the 6,000 years correspond to the six days of Creation, to such an extent that:

> Every little detail that occurred on these days will have its corresponding event happen at the proportionate time during its millennium. (*Biur HaGR"A, Safra D'Tzniusa*, Ch. 5)

This means that nothing happens randomly in history, but rather, all events can be traced back to a similar one that occurred during the six days of Creation. For example, if something happened in the first millennium, it is rooted in the first day of Creation. If it happened in the second millennium, then it is rooted in the second day of Creation, etc.

Hence, though history seems to randomly evolve, in reality, it is following a script that was written during the six days of Creation. In fact, history really does repeat itself, perhaps in ways we don't become aware of until after the fact, until it is too late.

Knowing this point is crucial for understanding just how historical our period of history is, and how dramatic the events of this time really are.

Tammuz 10

DAY SEVEN:
The Tenth Hour

Based upon the previous lesson, the sixth day of Creation is the basis for all that has happened in this millennium until now, and all that will happen until Year 6000. Therefore, if Adam and Chava ate from the *Aitz HaDa'as Tov v'Rah* on the sixth day of Creation, there will come a time, during the sixth millennium, that will correspond to that precise moment.

We know from the Talmud that Adam ate from the forbidden fruit during the tenth hour of Day Six (*Sanhedrin* 38b). And, as the *Leshem* explains:

> In *Pirkei d'Rebi Eliezer*, it says that one day for The Holy One, Blessed is He, corresponds to 12 hours of the day ... Since no creating occurred at night ... as it says in *Bereishis Rabba* (12:14). (*Sha'arei Leshem*, p. 270)

> [Therefore,] one hour [of a day of Creation] corresponds to 83 years and four months [of a millennium]. (Ibid. p. 289)

This would mean that, in 1990, or 5750 according to the Jewish calendar, history entered the "tenth hour" of history, an 83.33-year period of time that corresponds to the hour during which Adam *HaRishon* made the fateful mistake for which we are still paying! If ever there was a time to rectify the sin of mankind, this is the period of history in which to do it.

Ironically, the Internet, a modern-day version of the Tree of Knowledge of Good and Evil, and one of the greatest tests of our generation, came on to the world stage around 1990. It was also just prior to this time that the U.S.S.R. collapsed, and millions of Jews were finally allowed to emigrate to other countries, including *Eretz Yisroel*.

The Persian Gulf War also began at that time, which served to enhance the relationship between the Americans and the Arab world, while adversely affecting the relationship between the Americans and the Jewish people. Does all of this have to do with the tenth hour of Day Six? If we are living in the "tenth hour" of the sixth millennium, surely this is the basis for all that is happening today, especially since the biggest test of this generation is with respect to *da'as*—knowledge.

In other words, it is not only 2008, but it is also 18 years into a period of time that corresponds to when the first man made the most fatal error of history. Though we may not always understand how, this is the undercurrent for all that is happening at this time, which sheds new light, a more messianic light, on what seems to be an increasingly dark era.

It should inspire us to take the events of our history, and the role we can play in its making, far more seriously, especially in light of this next lesson. We are living in a very dramatic time.

Dedicated by Dr. and Mrs. Barry Shapero

DAY EIGHT:
How Much Time Really?

> I believe with perfect faith that there will be a resurrection of the dead, when the Creator, blessed is He, decides it is time … (Principle #13, *The Thirteen Principles of Faith*)

Just like a Jew must believe in the coming of *Moshiach* and the Final Redemption, he must likewise believe that there will be a resurrection of the dead. That is when God will create each person anew from the ground, as He did the first man.

Tradition explains that this stage of history is necessary in order to restore man back to his former spiritual glory. Apparently, eating from the *Aitz HaDa'as Tov v'Rah* caused man to become more physical, too physical to pass over into the next stage of existence after the year 6000. Resurrection will make each person as Adam *HaRishon* existed before the sin, with "skin of light" (*Sha'arei Leshem*, p. 352).

Therefore, the question has never been if there will be a period of resurrection, but when it will occur. According to many opinions, the appropriate time to resurrect the bodies of the dead is after the year 6000, in preparation for the final judgment, spoken about in the Talmud (*Sanhedrin* 99a).

However, this is not the opinion of all Torah commentators:

> There will be many resurrections, from the first one after the 40 years of *Kibbutz Golios*, to the last one at the end of a period of, according to Rebi Yehudah, 210 years ... according to Rebi Yitzchak, 214 years ... (*Midrash Ne'elam, Toldos* 140a) ... The period of *Techiyas HaMeisim* will be until the end of the 6000 years. (*Sha'arei Leshem*, p. 492)

If the Zohar is correct, then *Techiyas HaMeisim* is destined to begin either in 5786, according to Rebi Yitzchak, 18 years from now, or, according to Rebi Yehudah, in 5790, 22 years from now. Either way, according to both opinions, the resurrection of the dead will occur long before 6000.

This reduces the period of time, during which *Moshiach* must come, from 232 years, to at least 22 years, not a lot of time. This is because *Moshiach* will serve no use in *Techiyas HaMeisim*, since evil will have long ago been annihilated, and mankind will become more angel-like at that time (*Bava Basra* 75b).

Eighteen years into the "tenth hour" of history, a period of time that corresponds to when Adam *HaRishon* ate from the *Aitz HaDa'as Tov v'Rah*. Eighteen, to 22 years away from the end of *Yemos HaMoshiach*, when *Techiyas HaMeisim* will begin. This does not leave much time to transform the world into the utopian state described by the prophets of the past.

However, it does explain, perhaps, current historical trends. It certainly allows us to look at the events of recent history from a more Biblical perspective, since they might be the fulfillment of End-of-Days prophecies, something we have to do if want to be a partner with God in bringing the redemption—*peacefully*.

Dedicated Anonymously

Tammuz 12

DAY NINE:
The Pursuit of Holiness

God told Moshe, "Speak to the entire congregation of the Children of Israel and tell them, 'Be holy, for I, your God, am holy.'" (Vayikra 19:1-2)

As the *Ramban* points out, for the Jew, it is not enough just to be observant of the *mitzvos*. We have to be holy as well. This means, that we are supposed to pursue holiness at all times, to the best of our ability, as much as our circumstances permit.

If you had the choice to *doven* in a *shul* or in an airport, which would you choose? Most likely a *shul*, because a *shul* supports activities like prayer, whereas airports do not. Likewise, if you had to pursue holiness, where would you choose to do so, ideally-speaking, in *Eretz Yisroel*, or the Diaspora?

If you answered the Diaspora, consider the following:

> … All of this is the result of His holy light that emanates out from, and dwells next to, the *Kosel HaMa'arvi* — the Western Wall. From there it goes out and dwells amongst the Jewish people. (*Sha'arei Leshem*, p. 87)

In other words, the light of God does not descend on the rest of the world as it does over *Eretz Yisroel*. Rather, it descends over *Eretz Yisroel*, and then moves out in all directions to the rest of the world. The *kedushah* is strongest in *Eretz Yisroel*, because the opening to Heaven follows the borders of *Eretz Yisroel*, and does not extend beyond them (*Tuv HaAretz*, p. 2)

This is what Ya'akov *Avinu* realized after his dream, when he saw the angels of the Diaspora descend over *Eretz Yisroel*. He knew that the Temple Mount was holy; that is why he returned to pray there. Yet, after he awoke from his amazing dream, he stated emphatically:

> *"How awesome is this place! It is none other than the house of God, and this is the gate of heaven."* (*Bereishit* 28:7)

That is, *Eretz Yisroel* is the gate to Heaven, and nowhere else is in the world. Previously, Ya'akov had thought that all light flows up and down over each particular country, including Padan Aram to where he was headed for the next 20 years. After his dream, he understood that this is only so over *Eretz Yisroel*.

This meant, he realized, that any *kedushah* he would generate, from learning Torah and the performance of *mitzvos*, would have to first travel from Mesopotamea to *Eretz Yisroel* before ascending to Heaven, and that any blessing meant for him, would have to travel from *Eretz Yisroel* to Padan Aram, before reaching him.

This, we will see, has major implications.

L'Iluy Nishmas
Tuvia Leib ben David Avraham, z"l
(Ted Dvorkin)

Miriam bat Velvel, z"l
(Miriam Dvorkin)
Aryeh Chaim ben Tuvia Leib, z"l
(Richard Dvorkin)

May their memories be for a blessing.
Rena Cohen

Tammuz 13

DAY TEN:
The Problem with *Chu"l*

It says in *Tuv HaAretz*, in the name of the *Arizal*, the following:

> Even if a Jew who resides in *Chutz L'Aretz* performs Torah and *mitzvos* with as much purity as he can, nevertheless, the spirituality generated as a result will end up providing spiritual power to the ministering angel of that country. (*Tuv HaAretz, Ma'alas Eretz Yisroel v'Yeshivta*, p. 63)

He also explains that the only angel that is holy is the one responsible for overseeing *Eretz Yisroel*. The angel overseeing every other nation is from the side of impurity, which means that all *kedushah* generated in *Chutz L'Aretz* is handled by the impure angels along the way to *Eretz Yisroel*, before it can finally ascend to Heaven.

The problem is, that being the case, our *kedushah* in the Diaspora can end strengthening the side of impurity, which, as Ya'akov *Avinu* understood, works against us. This was totally unacceptable to him, but having no choice but to continue on his journey, he solved the problem by making a vow, saying:

> *"If God will be with me, and take care of me on the path I am going, and give me bread to eat and clothes to wear, and then*

bring me back in peace to my father's house, then God will be my God. (Bereishis 28:20-21)

In other words, Ya'akov *Avinu* was asking God to go with him into exile, and to protect him, and more importantly, the *kedushah* he would generate while living with his father-in-law, Lavan, one of the most impure men to ever live. This way, the side of impurity would never have more access to his holiness than is normally fitting, as if he had never left *Eretz Yisroel* in the first place, somewhat.

This is why we don't learn Torah or do holy things, like make *brochos*, in impure places. It is not just that it isn't fitting to perform such holy activities in such unholy places. It is also that such places are the home of the forces of impurity, and generating *kedushah* there only serves to strengthen them, increasing evil in Creation.

However, to be in a holy environment is to be surrounded by the *Shechinah*, which envelopes the *kedushah* we create with its own holiness, protecting it from the *Klipos*, or spiritual impurities. This keeps the world safe, even while the Jewish people are in the Diaspora, and allows us to flourish as a nation.

The only problem arises, when the Jewish people stay in the Diaspora longer than the *Shechinah*. Lacking spiritual protection, the *kedushah* we generate in the Diaspora is handled once again by the side of impurity, strengthening it, as seems to be the case today, and we must know how to respond.

Dedicated by Mr. & Mrs. Steve Weiser

Tammuz 14

DAY ELEVEN:
When The *Shechinah* Leaves

No believing Jew wants to live where the *Shechinah* is not. We have seen what happens to the Jewish people when we stay anywhere too long, which, according to our long and difficult history, seems to have been the case far too many times.

The question is, what does it mean to stay anywhere too long? It's almost impossible not to. Very often, though we begin in poverty, over time we tend to be successful in foreign countries, physically, spiritually, and emigrating then seems to be out of the question. With so much invested in our host countries, how does one simply move on?

But do we really have a choice, when staying too long has always meant losing all of that which we worked so hard to build up? Wouldn't it be better to leave our present homes, if the *Shechinah* is leaving, and while it is still safe?

According to Ya'akov *Avinu*, the answer is, yes. The moment he realized that the *Shechinah* was moving on, he didn't waste a single second; he simply went home, packed up his family, and headed out, not even saying good-bye to his father-in-law. *Doven* one more *Minchah* when the *Shechinah* is not there to protect the *kedushah*? Learn some Torah and feed the side of impurity? Not a chance.

The question is, how did Ya'akov know that the *Shechinah* was on the way out? The Torah answers that question as well:

> *[Ya'akov] heard Lavan's sons saying, "Ya'akov has taken everything that belonged to our father; from our father he has gained so much." When Ya'akov saw Lavan in person, he didn't behave with him as before.* (Bereishis 31:1-2)

Until that time, Lavan and his sons had behaved sufficiently well towards Ya'akov, but not because they were nice people, but because God protected Ya'akov from them. Like a wall, God protected Ya'akov from any anti-Semitism that was inherent in Lavan and his sons.

Therefore, when they started to display less-than-cordial appearances to Ya'akov, he took it as a sign that the *Shechinah* was reducing its protection, because the *Shechinah* was leaving Padan Aram. As a result, he decided that he must do so as well, and the sooner the better.

As history shows, anti-Semitism follows the Jewish people everywhere we go. It is not racism, because it can be the fiercest in places that the Jewish people have the lowest Jewish profile. It is actually supernatural, because it is a message from Heaven that an exile is coming to an end, so be ready. If the world is becoming less hospitable to the Jews, it is time to consider the possibility that the exile is coming to an end.

Dedicated by Dr. David Berman

Tammuz 15

DAY TWELVE:
Why *Eretz Yisroel*?

*I am God, your God, Who took you out of the land of Egypt,
to give you the land of Canaan, to be God to you. (Vayikra
25:38)*

Even for a Torah Jew who has yet to develop a yearning for *Eretz Yisroel* and the Final Redemption, *Eretz Yisroel* is the ultimate destination for all Jews. Whether we go before *Moshiach* comes, or after he comes, all Jews living in the time of *Moshiach* will end up there.

The question is, why is *Eretz Yisroel* so important to every Jew, aside from all of its intrinsic holiness? To begin with, it says:

> With respect to the Jewish people and *Eretz Yisroel*, the level of their souls, their Torah, and their relationship with God, is dependent upon their being in the Land of Israel. For the very soil of *Eretz Yisroel* is holy, the Jewish people are holy, their souls are holy, their Torah is holy, and God, their Minister, is holy. (*Tuv HaAretz, Ma'alas Eretz Yisroel L'Asid Lavo*, p. 34)

It is only in *Eretz Yisroel* that a Jew can truly achieve completion. He can be happy in *Chutz L'Aretz* for a time, but he can only really achieve completion in *Eretz Yisroel*.

Just as the holy Torah and *Eretz Yisroel* have a unique relationship, so too do the Jewish people have a unique and deep spiritual relationship to the Land of Israel. This is seen from the prophet Yechezkel (Ch. 48), when dividing up the land amongst the Twelve Tribes, granting each tribe the portion of land best suited for its needs. Thus, each tribe was bordered by the place from which the soul of his tribe emanated, and each *mitzvah* performed in *Eretz Yisroel* ascends and adorns each of the borders in relationship to the soul of each tribe. Hence, the completion of the soul is dependent upon which portion of land it dwells in, and the fulfillment of the land is dependent upon the souls that live there in a manner that is consistent with its very existence. (Ibid. p. 35)

Thus, we see, that there is an inescapable connection between the soul and the Land of Israel. Indeed:

The essence of *Torah Sh'b'al Peh* is within it. *(Pri Tzaddik, Parashas Massey 4)*

The goal of inheriting a portion of *Eretz Yisroel* has been to help each Jew find his own portion within *Torah Sh'b'al Peh*. *(Zohar Chadash* 2:137b)

These sources alone should be reason enough to make a Torah Jew yearn to live in *Eretz Yisroel*, and to anticipate the redemption. However, as we shall see, there are many others as well.

Masa Rivka Bat Hinda
Chai-Toubeh Bat Hinda

Three people who are essential to our family!
Mr. & Mrs. Lenny Solomon

Tammuz 16

DAY THIRTEEN:
Toras Eretz Yisroel

The Midrash states:

> There is no wisdom like the wisdom of *Eretz Yisroel*. (*Bereishit Rabbah* 16)

> The air of *Eretz Yisroel* makes a person wise. (*Bava Basra* 158b)

There are Kabbalistic reasons why this is so, but does it really matter in the end? All that matters is that it is true, and that the Jewish people are pursuers of wisdom. Knowledge can be acquired anywhere in the world, but wisdom, *Chazal* are teaching, is best acquired in *Eretz Yisroel*, as the Talmud states:

> Ten measures of wisdom fell to the world, nine of which fell on *Eretz Yisroel*, and one on the rest of the world. (*Kiddushin* 49b)

The *Malbim,* on Mishlei, explains that *chochmah,* is not something that one can learn on his own. Whereas knowledge can be self-taught, and is a function of human experience, wisdom is something that must be transmitted by God Himself. For, wisdom goes beyond anything that can be conveyed through the facts of experience.

In other words, it is a gift from God, a function of *Hashgochah Pratis*, something that is far more pronounced in *Eretz Yisroel*. As mentioned previously, the gate to Heaven is over *Eretz Yisroel* only, which means all blessing flows first to *Eretz Yisroel*, before heading out to the rest of the world.

Even though, geographically-speaking, *Eretz Yisroel* is on the face of the same earth as any other land, according to Kabbalah, it actually corresponds to a higher level in the *sefiros* than other lands. This is why when one travels to *Eretz Yisroel* he is said to always ascend (*Kiddushin* 69b), even though *Eretz Yisroel* is not the highest land in the physical world.

As light leaves one level of the *sefiros* for another level, lower down, it is filtered, reducing its intensity. And, since this light is the conveyor of Divine wisdom, the lower down a level is in the system, the less wisdom it will receive. Hence, the Talmud's statement:

> Ten measures of wisdom fell to the world, nine of which fell on *Eretz Yisroel*, and one on the rest of the world.

This is manifested in the physical world by the intrinsic holiness something or some place will have over other places. Hence, to yearn for wisdom, something that every Jew must do, since it is wisdom that enhances one's relationship with God, is to yearn for *Eretz Yisroel*. To yearn for *Eretz Yisroel* means to yearn for redemption, for the light and wisdom of *Eretz Yisroel* is greatly enhanced when the Jewish people live together on the land, and the *Bais HaMikdosh,* the Temple, is among us.

Dedicated in loving memory of
Yitzchak Ya'akov ben Yosef Dov Behr, z"l

Jack & Betty Winston

Tammuz 17

DAY FOURTEEN:
E"Y and *Olam HaBah*

Whatever we accomplish in this world, ultimately, it is for the sake of becoming a *Ben Olam HaBah*—someone who is guaranteed a good portion in the World-to-Come. Although it is true that every Jew is born with a portion in the World-to-Come (*Sanhedrin* 90a), one can increase or decrease that portion, depending upon how one behaves in this world.

Therefore, just as a Jew must pursue holiness to the best of his or her ability, he or she must also try to maximize his or her opportunity to earn reward in the World-to-Come. And, this is something, according to the *gemora*, that is much easier to do in *Eretz Yisroel*.

> Three inherit the World-to-Come: One who lives in *Eretz Yisroel* … (*Pesachim* 113a)

What is it about *Eretz Yisroel* that makes this so, and the following as well?

> Three wonderful gifts were given by The Holy One, Blessed is He, to the Jewish people, and all of them were given through hardship. They are Torah, *Eretz Yisroel*, and the World-to-Come. (*Brochos* 5a)

The answer is in the *gemora* itself, which states that:

> One who lives in *Eretz Yisroel* lives without transgression.
> (*Kesuvos* 111a)

How can that be? Just living on the land is not enough to prevent a person from actually committing a sin. In fact, there are extra *mitzvos* to do specifically with living on the land, such a *ma'aser* and *Shmittah*, that increase the possibility of sinning!

> *Eretz Yisroel* only atones for sins committed accidentally. For those done intentionally, suffering is necessary and a change of action. For wanton transgressions, only *teshuvah* and Torah can bring atonement. (*Tuv Ha'Aretz, Ma'alas Hadar b'Eretz Yisroel v'Pagam Hadar B'Chutz L'Aretz*, p. 70)

Remarkably, Rabbi Moshe Cordevero goes one step further and says that *Eretz Yisroel* atones for all types of sins, everyday of the year, providing that someone does not sin for this reason. In other words, a person can't say, "I will sin, since the land will atone for me," because it will not in such a case.

He explains that, if the land does not throw someone out, then they retain the name "*tzaddik*"—even if they don't appear that way to us. How much more so is this the case for someone who lives in *Eretz Yisroel* and tries to be righteous!

From all of this, one thing is clear: a person who wants to be a *Ben Olam HaBah* should certainly yearn to live on the only land in the world, about which the *gemora* says, a person earns eternal reward just by walking a distance of six feet (*Kesuvos* 111a)!

Hatzlacha rabba to Rabbi Winston for this important project. May he continue to have the strength to educate the world and that everyone should continue to benefit from his wisdom.

Steven Weiss

Tammuz 18

DAY FIFTEEN:
E"Y and *Bitachon*

Bitachon means "trust", and it usually refers to trust in God specifically. When life goes according to plan, and we feel a significant amount of control over the outcome of the events that matter a lot to us, there is very little room for *bitachon*, or so it seems. However, what choice do we have, but to turn to God for help, when we lack such control, and feel at the mercy of Divine Providence?

Is that a good thing, or a bad thing? On one hand, the Talmud teaches that:

> Rav Yannai [acted] upon his views, for he said, "A man should never stand in a place of danger and say that a miracle will happen for him, in case it doesn't. Even if a miracle does happen for him, it is deducted from his merits." (*Shabbos* 32a)

which says that one must not rely upon miracles to solve his problems.

On the other hand, it says:

> One who trusts in God will be surrounded by kindness (*Tehillim* 32:10). Even an evil person who trusts in God will be surrounded by kindness. (*Midrash Tehillim* 32:10)

This says that, if one does rely completely on God, miracles will happen for him. How is such a contradiction resolved? The answer has to do with the concept of *bitachon* itself.

As with any relationship, trust in God reveals the depth of the relationship one has with the Creator. The deeper the relationship, the more a person is prepared to trust the other person. The more one trusts the other person, the deeper the relationship becomes, and the Jewish people are all about developing and maintaining a close relationship with God.

When the need to rely upon God is a direct result of doing that which brings one closer to God, like taking off time from work to learn Torah when doing so seems to reduce much needed *parnassah*, then it is a *mitzvah* to rely upon God for success. There are countless stories of people who did this, and made up for lost wages in ways they never knew were possible.

However, when taking such risks is for selfish reasons, having little to do with God Himself, then it is considered negligent, and truly dangerous. Then it can result in tragic failure in this world, or a reduction of reward in the next world.

Eretz Yisroel is "*Eretz Bitachon*". It is a land of Divine Providence, because it is land that promotes closeness to God. It is a land that seems to say, "*How much are you prepared to rely upon God?*" since many times the solutions to problems are unconventional by Western standards, often coming at the last minute.

It often tests people to their limits, in order to push them to higher levels of spiritual greatness.

Hence, to live in *Eretz Yisroel* is not an issue of relying upon miracles. It is an expression of one's desire for closeness to God, and the extent to which he is prepared to go to achieve it. It may be a struggle, but it is precisely that struggle that indicates a Jew's resolve to adhere to God as much as he can. And that, ultimately, is the source of one's portion in the World-to-Come.

In memory of our dear mother,

Zoya Yusupov, z"l

Alex and Albert Yusupov

Tammuz 19

DAY SIXTEEN:
E"Y and *Achdus*

The fact that God allowed the second Temple to be destroyed because of *sinas chinum*—unwarranted hatred (*Avodah Zarah* 9b)—makes a strong case for the importance of *achdus*—unity—to the safety and the future of the Jewish people. How much more so is this true if receiving the Torah was predicated on the Jewish people reaching the level of "*k'ish echad b'leiv echad*"—like a single person with a single heart (*Rashi, Shemos* 19:2).

In fact, according to the *Shem M'Shmuel*, it had been Balak's and Bilaam's intention to only keep a fraction of the Jewish people from settling *Eretz Yisroel*. They understood that, had the entire nation settled the land together, this would have ushered in the Messianic Era, ridding the world of all evil (*Parashas Balak*).

Indeed, so integral to *geulah shlaimah* is *achdus* that the *navi* Yechezkel, in the *Haftarah* for *Parashas Vayigash*, defines the final redemption in terms of the unification of all Jews, ever since Yosef and his brothers first struggled against one another:

> *Thus said the Lord Hashem/Elohim: "Behold, I am taking the Children of Israel from among the nations to which they have gone; I will gather them from all around and I will bring them*

to their soil; I will make them into one nation in the land,
upon the mountains of Israel, and one king will be a king for
all of them; they will no longer be two nations, and they will
no longer be divided into two nations, ever again ... My ser-
vant Dovid will be king over them, and there will be one
shepherd for all of them ... (Yechezkel 37:21-24)

The lack of unity amongst the Jewish people does not reflect favorably on Torah, or even on the unity of God Himself. On the other hand, when the nations see the Jewish people acting and living as one people, according to one Torah, then it sanctifies the Name of God tremendously.

National unity is not going to happen in the Diaspora. The only place in the world that the Jewish people can achieve such sublime unity is in *Eretz Yisroel*, and not just because it is our homeland, but also because of its incredible spiritual qualities that allow each individual Jew to achieve personal completion. Only fulfilled Jews can bond with one another until they truly become, in the words of the Talmud, guarantors for one another (*Sanhedrin* 27b).

Hence, when we yearn for *Eretz Yisroel* and the Final Redemption, we are also showing Heaven how much we appreciate the need to unify with the rest of our people. We exhibit our appreciation of the need to become *ish echad b'leiv echad*, which also enhances our own ability to connect to Torah for the right reasons.

We may have to wait for God Himself to gather all of our people from all around the world to *Eretz Yisroel*. However, to yearn for such a reality is something we can do on our own, in the here-and-now.

In honor of
Rav Yonatan & Devorah Adler
whose love and dedication to *Eretz Yisroel* is helping
to turn the dream of the geulah into reality.

Tammuz 20

DAY SEVENTEEN:
According to the Effort

Without a doubt, life is far more comfortable for the average Jew today than it was 100 years ago. Even poor people are often better off than the "average" Jew of Europe a century ago. Thank God, society is more affluent today than ever before, and the Jewish people are beneficiaries as well.

As a result, it is even easier to do many of the *mitzvos* that our ancestors struggled to fulfill. We have always been good at learning from our gentile neighbors techniques and skills that can be used to further the cause of Torah.

However, the Torah lifestyle has never been a numbers game. It is rarely an issue of quantity of *mitzvos*, and always an issue of quality of *mitzvos*. Indeed, *mitzvos* are a Divinely-designed way of helping us to earn more reward in the World-to-Come, the "currency" of which is *mesiras Nefesh*—self-sacrifice:

According to the struggle is the reward. (*Pirkei Avos* 5:26)

The measure of love in any relationship is the extent to which one is prepared to sacrifice his or her agenda for that of the person he or she cares about. It doesn't always have to be that way, but when it does, *mesiras Nefesh* for another person is a statement of connection, and of a desire for an even more intense relationship.

The sacrifices of God are a broken spirit. (Tehillim 51:17)

It means the same thing, that God cherishes our willingness to put aside our personal agendas for His. It is true: the currency of the World-to-Come is *mesiras Nefesh*, that is, all the efforts we made throughout the course of our lifetime to fulfill the will of God, to come closer to Him, to act as a partner with Him to fulfill the mandate of Creation.

If life in *Eretz Yisroel* seems like a struggle, it is not a coincidence (if God wanted to, He could change that in a moment). It may not be the land of materialistic opportunity, but it is certainly the land of spiritual opportunity. It is a land designed to make it as easy as possible for the Jew to maximize his portion in *Olam HaBah*, by requiring *mesiras Nefesh* that may not be so forthcoming in more affluent countries.

Amazingly, for those who keep Torah and live in *Eretz Yisroel*, there is often an increased sense of life force that drives them to accomplish even more, in spite of the struggles that they may deal with on a daily basis. Like a bird, thrown out of the nest by the mother bird for the first time, in order to learn how to fly, living in *Eretz Yisroel* teaches a Jew how to truly live according to the words of *Chazal*, *"according to the effort is the reward"*. And, to derive satisfaction from doing so.

Dedicated by Dr. & Mrs. Mark Ruberto

Tammuz 21

DAY EIGHTEEN:
Relating to Destiny

Ultimately, any desire a Jew has for *Eretz Yisroel* and redemption flows from his or her desire to fulfill the destiny of the Jewish people, and the world in general.

After being around for over 3300 years, many of which have not been pleasant ones, it is easy to understand how the Jewish people could have lost the forest for the trees. It is difficult to be focused on one's ultimate destiny when day-to-day survival is a major issue. And, without a sense of destiny, it is difficult for a Jew to yearn for either redemption or *Eretz Yisroel*.

The destiny of the Jewish people is spelled out by God just in advance of receiving the Torah:

> *"You have seen what I did to Egypt, and how I bore you on eagles' wings, and brought you to Myself. If you will obey My voice, and keep My covenant, then you will be unique to Me above all the nations, for all the earth is Mine. You will be a kingdom of priests to Me, a holy nation."* (*Shemos* 19:3-6)

This is the final status of the Jewish people, and none of it can be achieved without the redemption and without the complete return of the Jewish people to *Eretz Yisroel*. Exile wears down the Jewish people spiritually, sometimes through too much suffering, other times because of too much comfort.

As history has shown many times over, it is not enough just to perform the *mitzvos* and acts of loving kindness. While both guarantee additional reward in the World-to-Come, they do not guarantee safe passage from one period of history to the next. They do not guarantee a *geulah b'rachamim*.

> Why did He bring darkness upon them? Because there were wicked people amongst the Jewish people of that generation who had no desire to leave Egypt, and these died during the three days of darkness. (*Rashi, Shemos* 10:22)

It doesn't mean that they didn't do the *mitzvos*, or act kindly to one another. Only one flaw was mentioned, and that was, a lack of desire to leave exile and live in the Promised Land. In other words, they did not relate to the ultimate destiny of the Jewish people, and that made them unworthy of redemption, and of life.

Amazingly, the death of 12,000,000 Jews is not recorded anywhere in the Torah. We only learn about it from the Midrash, which makes one wonder, how could the Torah leave out such an overwhelming detail, and relegate it to *midrash*? If, the death of just under 3,000 Jews in the incident of the golden calf is mentioned in the Torah, how much more so should the sudden death of 12,000,000 Jews be mentioned!

It's as if the Torah is saying, "If you're not plugged into the ultimate destiny of the Jewish people, it's as if you're not plugged in at all." It is very important, therefore, for a Jew to make sure that he never loses sight of the ultimate goals of the Jewish people.

In honor of my wife, Rachel bas Dovid HaLevi,
a true Ayshes Chayil.

Bruce Feinstein

Tammuz 22

DAY NINETEEN:
If Matzah Could Speak, 1

Why do we eat *matzah* at the *Seder*? To recall that the Jewish people had to leave Egypt so quickly that they didn't even have enough time to make provisions for their journey. There wasn't even enough time to let the dough they made rise and become bread, as the Torah states:

> They baked matzah from the dough they brought out of Egypt; it did not become leaven, since they were driven out of Egypt. For they could not delay, nor had they made provisions for themselves. (*Shemot* 12:39)

The real question is, why did the Jewish people have to leave Egypt so quickly? We know the answer to that question too: the Jewish nation had descended to the 49th level of spiritual impurity, and had they stayed a moment longer in the land of impurity, amongst such an impure people, they would have sunken down even further, to the 50th and final level of impurity. And, had that happened, then the descendants of Avraham, Yitzchak, and Ya'akov, would have forfeited the right to be redeemed.

Based upon this explanation, the *matzah* we eat each year at the *Seder* serves as a reminder of how close we came to spiritual oblivion, and how God miraculously saved us from such a terrible fate. Therefore, based upon this explanation, the *matzah* is a sign of celebration.

However, is it really? Perhaps we are overlooking some important details from the redemption story that effect the entire perspective, as the *Ba'al HaLeshem* writes:

> On the first night of Pesach, impurity had no power at all. It means just the opposite, for The Holy One, Blessed is He, emanated His holy light onto the Jewish people, as the author of the *Haggadah* has written, "The King of Kings was revealed to them" ... This is what the verse says, *"Egypt imposed itself upon the people, to quickly send them out of the land, for they said, 'We are all dying'."* (*Shemot* 12:33). (*Sha'arei Leshem*, p. 408)

In other words, by the time the 10th plague of the death of the firstborn occurred, the Jewish people had already left the Forty-Nine Gates of Spiritual Impurity, *completely*. Had they not, then they would not have sacrificed the *Korban Pesach*, and God certainly would not have revealed Himself to them.

Furthermore, the fact that the Egyptians were so broken reveals that impurity was weak, which means that *kedushah* was strong. On the night of the death of the first born, it was Pharaoh who went looking for Moshe and Aharon, and not the other around, proving that by the *Seder* that first Pesach night, there was no longer any danger to the Jewish people of sinking to the 50th gate of spiritual impurity.

So, why then did we have to leave so quickly?

Tammuz 23

DAY TWENTY:
If Matzah Could Speak, 2

If the Jewish people did not have to leave Egypt quickly to save themselves, then who were they saving? The *Leshem* explains:

> Therefore, they could not remain in Egypt a moment longer, since that would have eradicated the *S"A (Sitra Achra)* completely, and free-will, the true purpose of Creation, would have been eliminated. For, Egypt was the head of all the *Klipot,* and if she been destroyed, so then would have the *S"A*. The *yetzer hara* would have been destroyed completely, and free-will would no longer have existed. For this reason, they could not delay ... Therefore, they had to leave there quickly, in order that evil could continue to exist, so that free-will could still function, since it is the purpose of Creation. (*Sha'arei Leshem*, p. 408)

In other words, the danger of falling to the 50th gate of spiritual impurity was only in advance of the first plague of blood. That is, had God not sent Moshe *Rabbeinu* to save the Jewish people when He had, they would have descended to the spiritual point of no-return.

However, as each subsequent plague destroyed Egypt, being a revelation of God, it also re-built the Jewish people spiritually, until they left the gates of impurity altogether. By the first night of Pesach, the Jewish people had already entered the levels of holiness, and the light increased so quickly that it all but crushed all aspects of impurity, which had the effect of weakening Egypt.

However, for free-will to remain relevant, good and evil must co-exist. If good overpowers evil, as was the case in Egypt, then free-will stands to be eliminated. This was something that God could not accept at the time, even though, in *Yemos HaMoshiach*, it will finally be this way (*Succah* 52a). Nevertheless, at that time it was premature, and therefore evil had to be strengthened to allow free-will to continue to exist.

Only because, the *Leshem* explains, the Jewish people had never chosen redemption for themselves. God had imposed it upon them, to fulfill His promise to Avraham, Yitzchak, and Ya'akov. But, even as redemption came closer with each plague, the Jewish people never actually choose redemption for themselves.

Therefore, the *matzah* each year is a reminder of unfinished business. It may be a symbol of celebration, but it is also a symbol of what should have been, and wasn't. Thus, each year, as we focus on the *matzah* at the Seder table, we have to hear it ask us, *"Have you chosen redemption for yourself yet?"*

Dedicated by Alvin & Yehudis Schamroth

Tammuz 24

DAY TWENTY-ONE:
We Pray For It

Of the many activities that the Jewish people do most, prayer is certainly one of them. And, one of the most difficult aspects of prayer is remaining focused on the words and their meanings, especially after having said the same words so many times before.

Thus, it is easy to have forgotten that so many aspects of the daily *Shemonah Esrai* deal with the concept of redemption. In fact, Rabbi Yechezkel Levenstein, the famed *Mashgiach Ruchani* of the Mir Yeshiva and Ponovez Yeshiva, said it this way:

> When it comes to the arrival of *Moshiach* and the resurrection of the dead, we are quiet, as if we are embarrassed to speak about them, as if we have given up them altogether ... In truth, almost the majority of the *Shemonah Esrei* deals with the future redemption ... and, just as we are lacking faith in this matter, we are also distant from the essence of prayer. We lack connection to [the blessings regarding redemption], and all of our prayers are only lip service! (*Ohr Yechezkel, Emunas HaGeulah*, 1960; p. 287)

These are strong words, but for many, they might ring true. If so much of the *Shemonah Esrai* is devoted to helping us maintain a redemption-oriented consciousness, wouldn't it be inconsistent to pray them and not try and take them seriously?

When the *Anshei Knesses HaGadolah,* the Men of the Great Assembly, established the prayer service, they weren't just telling us what to pray, they were also telling us what we should remain conscious of, even when not praying. They wanted prayer to be a time of regaining a clarity of the issues that matter most to the Jew, because they knew that exile can be very distracting.

Hence, as the rabbis point out, the word "to pray" is reflexive: *l'hispalel.* For, prayer is an internal journey into deeper levels of one's consciousness, in order to get in touch with one's inner self, and what truly counts to him. All day long mundane concerns pursue us and steal our attention. At least during *tefillah,* we are required to push them all aside, in order to get back to spiritual basics.

Therefore, in order to enhance *tefillah* in a general sense, it is a worthwhile use of time to sit down and consider the meaning of the words, what they mean to you, and what they should mean to you. During *Shemonah Esrai* is not the time to do this, because it is easy for the mind to go off on tangents, as one thought leads to another. At that time, as a person stands before God in *Shemonah Esrai,* he or she should already be clear about what to think about.

Therefore, these next few lessons will focus on the *brochos* of the *Shemonah Esrai,* particularly those that speak about redemption-related concepts. Not only will this enhance the prayer experience in general, but it will provide insight into how to enhance one's yearning for redemption from the words themselves.

Dedicated by Mr. & Mrs. Erwin Cymet

Tammuz 25

DAY TWENTY-TWO:
Giver of Knowledge

The fourth blessing of the *Shemonah Esrai* is, "*Chonain Da'as*", which blesses God for giving man, knowledge, understanding, and the power of discernment. We may not take *Da'as* for granted, since it allows man to accomplish so many positive things in life, but we do tend to forget where it comes from. Therefore, from the beginning, we thank God for it.

The Talmud emphasizes the importance of *Da'as* by stating, in reference to this *brochah*:

> Rebi Elazar said: Anyone who has *dayah*, it's as if the Temple was built in his day ... (*Brochos* 33a)

The *gemora* makes this statement based upon a *drash*, but obviously wouldn't if there wasn't a strong connection between the two. The question is, how is something as basic as *dayah* so important that it can be considered as if the *Bais HaMikdosh* was built just because a person possesses it?

The answer comes in the form of a *mishnah* from *Pirkei Avos*, and by understanding the essence of man. It says:

> *"The tablets were made by God, and the writing was God's writing, engraved (charus) on the tablets"* (Shemos 32:16). Do not read *"charus"*—engraved—but rather *"chairus"*—freedom—for no one is free except the one who learns Torah. (*Pirkei Avos* 6:2)

What does it mean to be free? It means having the opportunity to fulfill yourself, in order to reach your ultimate potential. The *yetzer hara* interferes with that, by convincing us to pursue unworthy goals, or less worthy ones, in order to keep us from making the most out of our lives. We were given free-will to combat that.

Torah allows us to be clear about our personal goals, and the ultimate goals of the Jewish people. That knowledge alone is what gives a person the spiritual fortitude to make tough, but ultimately meaningful decisions in life. They may not be the most comfortable choices to make at the time, but in the end, they are the most gratifying ones.

This is the connection to the *Bais HaMikdosh*. The *Bais HaMikdosh* is the symbol of all the aspirations of the Jewish people, the long-term objectives of the Jewish nation: *dveikus Hashem*—closeness to God. When one identifies with the former, he automatically identifies with the latter, and vice-versa.

It takes *da'as* to do that. It takes *Da'as Elokim*—Godly knowledge—to recognize what the ultimate goals of the Jewish people are, and how to achieve them. This puts a person on track with the building of the third and final temple, and though it may not happen in his day, from Heaven's point of view, it is as if it did.

Dedicated by Katrin Levy

Tammuz 26

DAY TWENTY-THREE:
Redeemer of Israel

The seventh blessing says:

Please see our suffering, take up our fight, and redeem us speedily for Your Name's sake, for You are a powerful redeemer ...

How easy it must have been to be sincere about this *brochah* during the Crusades, or the many pogroms we had to persevere, and certainly during the Holocaust. How difficult it has become for many in our generation to say these words with conviction when we are better off, materialistically, than all the generations before us. Even performing *mitzvos* is easier to do in this generation.

So what about the *brochah*? Is it a time-oriented blessing, that only applies to Jews in distress? Perhaps this is why *Chazal* built into the *brochah* the words, "redeem us speedily for Your Name's sake", for that remains an urgent and unfulfilled need the entire time the Jewish people are in exile, whether we suffer or prosper.

The *Nefesh HaChaim* (2:11) explains why we pray for the recovery of fellow Jews who are ill. "*So they don't have to be sick!*" we may think to ourselves. However, it is not so simple, especially since, as the Talmud says, every suffering is a *tikun*. Do we know when a person's *tikun* should end, and when it should not?

Of course not. Yet, we pray for the *refuah shlaimah* of Jews anyhow, because, as the *Nefesh HaChaim* explains, it is a *Chillul Hashem*, a profanation of God's holy Name, when Jews suffer. It makes it appear to us and the rest of the world as if God isn't involved in our lives, or that He doesn't care about us if He is.

Therefore, when we pray for the recovery of an ill Jew, we are actually praying for the *Chillul Hashem* to end. It's not that we are not concerned about the well-being of our fellow Jew; we most definitely are. However, not knowing what is good or bad for our fellow Jew, especially if God sees fit to inflict him, it is hard to ask for the illness to be removed if it is for the good of the Jew who is unwell.

However, as the *Tikunei HaZohar* points out (*Tikun* 6, 22a), if we suffer, then the *Shechinah* is suffering, and therefore we must pray for the Divine Presence before we pray for anything else. For, if the *Shechinah* is "unwell", then impurity grows in strength, and holiness suffers, and you can't have a greater *Chillul Hashem* than this.

If this is true about illness, how much more so must this be true if the Jewish people remain in exile, with little or no hope of being redeemed in the immediate future? And, the fact that Jews seem to be happy in exile only compounds the matter, and therefore, we pray: if we can't appreciate the need for redemption for our own sake, then do it for Your sake, to end the *Chillul Hashem*, so that the words, "*On that day, He will be one and His Name, one*" (*Zechariah* 14:9) can finally be fulfilled.

Thus, to yearn for redemption is to yearn for an end to the *Chillul Hashem* that is associated with exile. In fact, the prophet says, regarding the Final Redemption, exactly this:

> *Thus said God: It is not for your sake that I act, O House of Israel, but for My Holy Name that you have desecrated among the nations where you came. I will sanctify My great Name that is desecrated among the nations, that you have desecrated among them; then the nations will know that I am God—the word of God—when I become sanctified through you before their eyes. I will take you from among the nations and gather you from all the lands, and I will bring you to your soil. (Yechezkel 36:21-24)*

Hence, though this blessing may be short, it is long on meaning. If our hearts don't break when reciting it, it is because we have become desensitized to the concept of *geulah*, and the gravity of *Chillul Hashem*.

This may not be something that can be repaired by simply saying the *brochah* each day. However, it has to be a step in the right direction, and will be, if we take its words to heart.

May the merit of the learning of this lesson
be for a *refuah shlaimah* of

Shayna bas Madelyn

and the health of

Baruch Berel ben Leiba

Norm & Marsha Smagley

Tammuz 27

DAY TWENTY-FOUR:
Blow the Shofar

The tenth blessing reads as follows:

Blow the great shofar for our freedom, and raise the banner to gather our exiles, and gather us together from the four corners of the earth ...

There is nothing complicated about this blessing; its message is succinct and clear. The Diaspora is not home, no matter how comfortable it may feel, and no matter how easy it may be to perform *mitzvos* while there. We long, at least we are supposed to, to find our way back from the four corners of the earth, to one location: *Eretz Yisroel.*

On the other hand, if a person says this blessing without conviction, hoping that its fulfillment will take place in another lifetime, just to avoid dealing with the issue of *aliyah* and a change of lifestyle, as well as location, then what does this blessing mean to him, or to God for that matter? In such a case, a person is asking for something he doesn't really want, so then why ask?

Well, we can't change the *nusach* of the *Shemonah Esrai,* so instead we have to change ourselves. In generations when poverty and anti-Semitism never allowed us to feel at home in foreign countries, we had little trouble being sincere about this blessing. However, now that both have sub-sided, *for the time being*, for many, the heart has difficulty being real about the words that flow from the mouth.

Chazal had the foresight to know that, in some genera-tions, this would be the case. Since many of *the Anshei Knesses HaGadolah* were prophets, they were already aware of what awaited world Jewry in advance of *Moshiach's* arrival. They composed these blessings specifi-cally so that we could ask ourselves during such confusing times, *"Is this brochah real to me, and if not, why not?"*

Perhaps, there is another meaning for the word *"neis"* here, which in the case translates as "banner". However, the word can also mean "miracle", and perhaps the rabbis who composed the *Shemonah Esrai* built into this blessing a request of a different nature as well: perform a miracle, and gather in the exiles, because that is certainly what it is go-ing to take to bring millions of Diaspora Jews home at this point!

Perhaps this is why the Vilna Gaon taught that the *mitzvah* of facilitating *Kibbutz Golios*, more than any other *mitzvah*, invokes great *siyita d'Shemaya*. Of all the *mitzvos* a Jew may perform, it can be one of the hardest to do and complete, ever since the Spies first rejected *Eretz Yisroel*.

In the meantime, when *dovening Shemonah Esrai*, don't just let these words roll off your lips into spiritual oblivion. Think about them, and try to get a sense of where you hold with them. In the end, you have to be as sincere about this blessing as you are regarding the ones to do with knowledge, forgiveness, health, and wealth.

Tammuz 28

DAY TWENTY-FIVE:
Return Our Judges

One of the signs that the Messianic Period is about to begin is when the governments of the world become corrupt (*Sanhedrin* 97a). The amazing thing is how much corruption can exist, and yet people can still go about their daily lives as if everything is normal—until such corruption touches their own personal lives.

However, Jewish leadership is judged by a much higher standard than that of the rest of the world, and therefore, it does not have to be an issue of corruption, just faulty judgment. As the Talmud states:

> If you see a generation that has many troubles, investigate the judges of Israel, since all punishment comes to the world because of the judges of Israel. (*Shabbos* 139a)

> The Holy One, Blessed is He, won't cause His *Shechinah* to dwell on the Jewish people until the evil judges and police cease from amongst them. (Ibid.)

Thus, we see, that even if we are fortunate enough not to have to go to court, and therefore fortunate enough not to have to be subjected to what may seem like an unfair judgment, either against us or another party, we are still affected. If punishment comes to the world because of bad judgments in *Bais Din*, we are affected. If the *Shechinah* can't dwell on the Jewish people because Jewish judges aren't doing as good a job in court as expected, then we are affected.

Hence, the wording of the *gemora* tells it all. It implies:

"Take a look around. How are things going for the Jewish people? Good? Bad? If bad, then take a look at the judges of your generation, if you haven't already done so until now. If there is suffering in the world, it has to do with the judges of Israel. Do something about it, if you want the suffering to end."

Like praying, for example, for better judges, as we do in the eleventh blessing of the *Shemonah Esrai*:

Restore our judges as in earliest times and our counselors as at first; remove from us sorrow and groan; and reign over us—You, God, alone—with kindness and compassion, and justify us through judgment.

Is this likely to happen in advance of *Moshiach's* arrival? Not likely, especially as life becomes increasingly more confusing, even for the religious Jew, as the time of the redemption approaches. Hence, even some of the greatest rabbis of the past are quoted as saying, "Let *Moshiach* come, but don't let me be there when it happens!"

They knew what to expect, what it would be like just prior to *Moshiach's* arrival, and feared it. Our ability to live through this period is not a measure of spiritual strength, but of our spiritual desensitization. Therefore, to say this blessing with sincerity shows Heaven how much we appreciate this, and yearn for better times.

Dedicated in memory of
Dovid Moshe Moss, z"l
Alfred & Goldie Tarren, z"l
Charles & Dorothy Moss, z"l
Ruth Cantor, z"l

Ahuvah Moss

Tammuz 29

DAY TWENTY-SIX:
Stop the Slanderers

The twelfth *brochah* is the reason why the *Shemonah Esrai*—the "Eighteen"—in fact, has 19 blessings. Added during Roman times, when Jews informed on fellow Jews who kept Torah in secret and at the risk of death, it has been relevant ever since:

> And for the slanderers let there be no hope; and may all wickedness perish in an instant; and may all Your enemies be cut down speedily. May You speedily, uproot, smash, cast down, and humble wanton sinners—speedily in our days.

Contemplating the words of this blessing, one can have a better appreciation of the pain of exile throughout the last few millennia. It is just in recent times, *thank God*, that the most of the Western world has acted more civilly towards the Jewish people, though, in some parts of the world, the Jewish people are still treated as second class citizens, if not worse.

And, whenever Jews are treated harshly, there are bound to be some who will try to escape the cruelty at the cost of safety to their fellow Jews. If we depend upon God for our safety even when we strong and secure, how much more so do we depend upon His Providence when we are weak and vulnerable.

However, today, this blessing has additional meaning as well, as some Jews make decisions on behalf of the Jewish nation that may, in fact, be reckless.

The world is a different place for a Jew who abandons Torah and instead, embraces a secular lifestyle. It is not long before he or she adopts a Western point of view, which often places the world's objectives at odds with the Torah objective for the Jewish people. When this happens, and such Jews are in positions of leadership, they can make decisions that please the world, but not God.

Furthermore, this has resulted in the establishment of courts and a legal system in *Eretz Yisroel* that is modeled after the Western systems. This has often resulted in rulings and actions that are often difficult for Torah Jews, not just in *Eretz Yisroel*, but for Jews all around the world.

For, as the Talmud states, every Jew is a guarantor for his fellow Jew (*Sanhedrin* 27b), and therefore shares his burden no matter where he may live in the world. Furthermore, we have already seen how Jewish judges affect the world in general, regardless of political and national boundaries, so the problem is a universal one, not just a local one.

Therefore, anyone who is sensitive to where the Jewish people stand today—80 percent assimilation and 52 percent intermarriage—should yearn for redemption to bring an end to this problem as well.

**Dedicated by Rabbi Winston's
Ramat Beit Shemesh Women's Shiur**

Av 1

DAY TWENTY-SEVEN:
Rebuild Jerusalem

Who would have thought that the world would want to divide Jerusalem, taking part of it away from the Jewish people? What could be more backwards in terms of the Final Redemption than this? However, as the fourteenth blessing teaches, it is not just about physically possessing Jerusalem, but possessing it spiritually as well:

> And, to Jerusalem, Your city, may You return in compassion, and may You rest within it, as You have spoken. May You re-build it soon in our days as an eternal structure, and may You speedily establish the throne of David within it.

Even though, in 1967, a miracle occurred that allowed the Jewish people to regain control over all of Jerusalem, *Har HaMoriah*—the Temple Mount—was permitted to re-main under the control of the Arab world. Not only do the Jewish people remain without a temple, we don't even pos-sess the place that it is supposed to stand, and have to watch while others desecrate the holiest place in the world with false forms of worship.

Even within the walls of the Old City itself, places exist and activities occur that are not in keeping with the holi-ness of the site. And, beyond the walls in the rest of the city, it is often difficult to remember that Jerusalem is supposed to be a city of God, which more than likely, has contributed, on a spiritual level, to the problem at hand.

We say:

> If I forget you, O Jerusalem, let my right hand forget its skill. Let me tongue cling to my palate if I don't remember you, if I don't place Jerusalem above my greatest joy. (Tehillim 137:5-6)

By writing this, Dovid *HaMelech* was trying to make us realize that success means nothing as long as Jerusalem is not living up to its spiritual potential. Even if a Jew lives in Jerusalem, but he still fails to appreciate how far the city is from existing on its ideal level of holiness, he has, by definition, forgotten Jerusalem as well.

Likewise, if we can recite this blessing without much intention, without really feeling the importance of its words, and what Jerusalem should mean to us, have we not also forgotten Jerusalem as well? Are we not inviting God to cause our right hand to forget its skill, and our tongue to cling to our palate, thereby denying us the pleasures of this world, and of the next world?

For, as the Talmud states:

> Rav Shmuel bar Nachmani said in the name of Rebi Yochanan: Three were called by the name of The Holy One, Blessed is He, and they are: righteous people, *Moshiach*, and Jerusalem ... (Bava Basra 75b)

Caring about Jerusalem, therefore, is a reflection of one's love of God. Yearning for it, and for the temple to be rebuilt, is one of the best indicators of how much a Jew wants to be close to his Creator.

L'illuy nishmat

Aliza bat Carl, z"l
(Ilza Jorden)

By her loving granddaughter's family,
The Turner Family
Ramat Bet Shemesh, Israel

Av 2

DAY TWENTY-EIGHT:
Offspring of David

The next blessing refers to *Moshiach* himself:

> The sprouting of Your servant David may You speedily cause to flourish, and enhance his pride through Your salvation, for we hope for Your salvation all day long.

The language of this blessing is not coincidental, but intentionally metaphoric. The comparison of the appearance of *Moshiach Ben Dovid* to a sprouting plant indicates that the process of redemption grows like a plant. For the most, its growth is imperceptible to our eyes, until all of a sudden, one day, in amazement, we see a completed plant.

Rabbi Shlomo Eliyashiv, the *"Leshem"*, says a similar thing:

> At the beginning *Yemos HaMoshiach*, there will be a combination of Nature and miracle working together at one time, as we saw during the redemption from Egypt. Then, also, at the beginning of the redemption, there were great miracles. Yet, the Jewish people remained quite physical and material ... Even though He dealt with them with great miracles, nevertheless, they themselves lived completely naturally. It will be likewise at the beginning of *Yemos HaMoshiach:* the redemption will also be with great miracles, but Nature will still

function as well; the physicality and materialism of the entire world will remain, as well as with respect to the Jewish people ... Rebi Yudan says: It is because the redemption for this people will not come all at once, but will progress over time ... For this reason, the redemption is compared to dawn, as it says, *"Then your light will burst out like the dawn"* (*Yeshayahu* 58:8); see there. (*Sha'arei Leshem*, p. 488)

When did the redemption from Egypt begin? When Moshe *Rabbeinu* was born? When God sent him the first time? The second time? When the plagues began? By *Rosh Chodesh Tishrei*, when they were finally able to stop showing up for work? We know exactly when they left Egypt, but that was already the end of the redemption process, not the beginning of it.

The point is that the redemption process is not an overnight one. It takes time, and can seem to move so slowly that it may even seem as if it is going backward, though it never does. Everything that has to get accomplished to fulfill the purpose of Creation gets done, one way or another, whether we notice it or not.

This is one of the reasons why a Jew must not only expect redemption, but even anticipate it:

In the blessing of *"Et Tzemach Dovid"* one should have intention with the words "for Your salvation we hope all day", that we long for the redemption, in order to fulfill one's obligation to long for the coming of *Moshiach*, [which is one of the first questions one will be asked by the Heavenly court after death]. (*Shulchan Aruch/Shaarei Teshuvah 118:1*)

One of the differences between the four-fifths who died in the Plague of Darkness and the one-fifth that left Egypt with Moshe *Rabbeinu*, was probably that the latter had been ready for redemption, and the former had not been. The one-fifth had grown redemption-oriented with the ongoing process, whereas the four-fifths still maintained an exile-mentality.

The Talmud says the following thing:

> Rebi Yehoshua ben Levi met Eliyahu standing by the entrance of Rebi Shimon bar Yochai's cave ... He then asked him, "When will *Moshiach* come?"
> He told him, "Go and ask him."
> "Where is he sitting?"
> "At the entrance to Rome."
> "How shall I recognize him?"
> "He is sitting among the poor lepers, and all of them untie [their bandages] at one time, and re-bandage them together, whereas he unties and re-bandages each separately, thinking, 'Should I be wanted, I must not be delayed'." (*Sanhedrin* 98a)

From this we see, the *Chofetz Chaim* wrote in his work, "*Tzepisa L'Yeshua*" that *Moshiach* can arrive at a moment's notice: those who are prepared for redemption will rejoice, whereas those who remain unprepared, may only become confused. Therefore, part of this blessing is a request to God to not only bring *Moshiach*, but to include us also in the process as well. At the very least, we should be able to see it happening and to take note of that which is occurring, and be able to understand how it helps the *geulah*-process reach its ultimate goal.

Dedicated by Margolit Katz

Av 3

DAY TWENTY-NINE:
Return the *Shechinah*

May our eyes see Your return to *Tzion* in mercy. Blessed are You, God, Who returns His Presence to *Tzion*.

This is the end game of all of our yearning and efforts. We may have lost track of this over the millennia of exile, but this is supposed to be the entire focus of the Jewish people, according to the *Tikunei HaZohar* (*Tikun* 6, 22a): returning the *Shechinah* to *Tzion*, as it was during the time of the first temple.

We learn from the *Mishkan* that, in spite of the tremendous effort by the Jewish people to build a dwelling place for God, it was worth little until the Presence of God actually descended to occupy it. Likewise, the entire Jewish nation could return to *Eretz Yisroel*, and even build a temple, but until the *Shechinah* descends to occupy it, the redemption is not complete.

But, isn't the *Shechinah* always here? Doesn't it even go into exile with the Jewish people? The answer is yes, but there is a big difference between the *Shechinah* being among the Jewish people in exile, and returning to *Tzion* itself. A huge difference.

For example, all of the success that the Jewish people enjoy while in exile, and all of the protection they may have, is the result of the *Shechinah* that is among them. Even the success of a host nation is the result of the *Shechinah* among the Jewish people. However, does that stop assimilation? Does it stop intermarriage? Does it prevent *Chillul Hashem*, and bring the gentiles, in whose lands we live, to righteousness? No, on all accounts.

However, during the period of the First Temple, there were times when nations came from far and wide to witness the wisdom of the Jewish people, and usually left somewhat transformed, and certainly impressed. We were, for periods of time, the "light unto nations" we were redeemed from Egypt to become (*Yeshayahu* 2:6).

It is hard to sanctify the Name of God when 80 percent of the Jewish people do not care for Judaism, especially when a significant portion of that 80 percent does not even care for the Jewish people and Israel at all. Nor, does it make a positive impression on anyone when the remaining one-fifth, the religious part of the Jewish people, has difficulty agreeing with one another on some very important issues.

And now, after many decades of being able to keep the Arabs and the world at bay, we have since lost parts of *Eretz Yisroel*, and other communities are slated for destruction. They are trying to divide Jerusalem, and construction has been halted in many of the areas that the Arabs are demanding from the Jewish people.

Furthermore, sickness seems to be affecting the Jewish people like never before. So many of the concerns that, in the past, seemed to only really affect the gentiles, are now becoming Jewish problems as well. This certainly gives the impression to many that God is no longer on the side of the Jewish people, a terrible *Chillul Hashem*.

But, not nearly one as bad as the Holocaust was, or any of the many pogroms that devastated entire communities across Europe and Asia through the centuries. Whereas once, the Jewish people were looked up to by so many gentile nations, today, those who adhere to Torah, barely command respect from anyone outside their own circle of influence.

All of this is the result of the *Shechinah* not having returned to *Tzion* as of yet. It is not all or nothing: the *Shechinah* will return to *Tzion* over time. However, until such time as the transition is complete, the world can become a volatile place, especially for the Jew, and especially for the Diaspora Jew.

We have plenty of reason to say this blessing daily, and with a lot of intention. Personal completion depends upon it, and certainly national completion does so as well.

Dedicated by Haddasa Levitan

Av 4

DAY THIRTY:
Bring Peace

The nineteenth blessing of the *Shemonah Esrai* is one for peace:

> Bring peace and blessing, grace, kindness, and mercy upon us and all of Israel, Your people. Bless us, our Father, all of us together with the light of Your face, because with the light of Your face, God our God, You gave us Torah of life, and love of kindness, righteousness, blessing, mercy, life, and peace, and may it be good in Your eyes to bless Your people Israel at all times and every hour with Your peace.

Of all the states of existence mankind has pursued since the beginning of his history, peace has been the most elusive. The cost has been tremendous.

It began with the murder of Hevel by his twin brother Kayin, and got worse over time. War after war has killed trillions of people over five-and-a-half millennia, and has devastated vast amounts of the world. The amount of wastage is too vast to describe, and no one has learned anything from past experience. We live on the brink of war once again.

Not only this, but the peace plan being imposed upon *Eretz Yisroel* and the Jewish people is anything but that, showing just how little mankind understands the concept of peace. It seems as if the people trying to bring it about either don't understand what it is, or if they know, they lack the courage to take the steps to make it a reality.

Thus, the final blessing of the *Shemonah Esrai* speaks not only of peace, but of God's peace, for, it seems, He is the only one who can bring it about. Apparently, to make true and lasting peace, one must have a far greater appreciation of the long term goals of humanity than any man has ever had, with the exception of a few great people. Only by knowing the future of mankind can he know how to steer in the present.

This is not only true on a national level, but on a personal level as well. Peace of mind does not only mean feeling a sense of calm, because someone can delude himself into achieving such a state of mind. True peace of mind has to exist after dealing with all of the important issues in life, not at the exclusion of awareness of them. Hence, self-honesty is also extremely important for inner peace.

The Talmud says, that ever since Adam *HaRishon* sinned and changed his spiritual status, the *yetzer hara* has been stronger than the *yetzer tov*, making it extremely easy to act immorally. If God doesn't help us against our *yetzer hara*, there will be no way to prevail (*Kiddushin* 30b).

Prevailing, therefore, depends very much upon realizing how dependent we are on God for all forms of peace, personal or international. And, by yearning for redemption, we show God how much we acknowledge our dependency, and it open the channels for Him to provide us with His idea of peace, the true and lasting version.

Yearning for redemption says, "I realize that, without You, we can't truly achieve peace, and that redemption is necessary to create the kind of situation that makes it possible for such Divine assistance, on such a grand scale." Without such a realization, peace remains elusive on all levels of life.

Av 5

DAY THIRTY-ONE:
Ideal State

It is often said that, "You don't know what you have until you lose it." If that is so, then it is certainly even more difficult to appreciate what you *can* have if you have never had it before. Why should we want better when we have it so good now, and have never known what "better" is like? To yearn for something, you have to first know what it is like.

All of the blessings of the *Shemonah Esrai* ask God to allow us to exist in an ideal state; we're asking Him to grant us everything we need to live a perfect life. In other words, we're praying for *Yemos HaMoshiach* to begin already, not just for God to enhance our everyday physical life in exile. It is this for which we are supposed to yearn daily.

But, how can you yearn for something you have never experienced? The truth is, we have, to some degree, at different points in history, tasted a little of what *Yemos HaMoshiach* is supposed to be like. We have witnessed periods of history when good has triumphed over evil to such a degree that people have believed that the Messianic Era was actually about to begin.

Even though the Talmud states:

There is no difference between this world and *Yemos HaMoshiach* other than the [lack of] oppression of nations. (*Brochos* 34b)

which means peace, at last, among the nations, it also says:

In the Time-to-Come, The Holy One, Blessed is He, will bring the *yetzer hara* and slaughter it before the righteous and the evil ... (*Succah* 52a)

In truth, the first result is dependent upon the second one, since world peace will not be possible until the *yetzer hara* is gone, and with it, all the negative human traits that breed controversy and war. As long as the *yetzer hara* is active, there will always be someone who will be willing to sacrifice morality for personal gain.

Thus, to yearn for the ideal state of mankind is to yearn for the period of history in which there is no *yetzer hara*, no strife, no jealousy, no anger—no ungodly traits whatsoever. It is to yearn for the time when the average person in the street will not be so average, but someone who truly reflects the inner Godliness with which man was first created. As a result, *mitzvos* will no longer be a challenge but the most natural way of life. Without a *yetzer hara* to create the possibility of rationalization, every individual will see the world as God does, and live accordingly. The world may function quite naturally still, at least in the beginning, but the entire concept of Nature will shift based upon new historical developments, as we will now discuss.

L'iluly Nishmas
a friend and colleague and a very special soul

Boruch ben Chayil, z"l
(Boruch Crowley)

who was a tremendous help with my original
web site and many projects.

Pinchas Winston

Av 6

DAY THIRTY-TWO:
Ideal Time

If the *yetzer hara* is eliminated during *Yemos HaMoshiach*, then so is the *Malach HaMaves*—the Angel of Death, as it says:

> Reish Lakish said: *Satan*, the *yetzer hara*, and the Angel of Death are all one. (*Bava Basra* 16a)

Does that mean that death will also be eliminated? No, as Rabbi Shlomo Eliyashiv, the *"Ba'al HaLeshem"* explains:

> Death will not come from the Angel of Death, *God forbid*, because he will have been eliminated completely, as it says: In the Time-to-Come, The Holy One, Blessed is He, will bring the *yetzer hara* and slaughter it before the righteous and the evil ... (*Succah* 52a). Then the world will be completely purified ... and the matter of death then will be through The Holy One, Blessed is He, alone ... as was the death of Moshe *Rabbeinu*, the deaths of the Forefathers, Aharon, and Miriam ... (*Drushei Olam HaTohu*, 2:4:12:9)

This is known as the concept of *"Neshikah"*, or *"Divine Kiss"*. According to the Talmud, there are 903 forms of death (*Brochos* 8a), of which *Neshikah* is the most pleasant of all of them. It is the way that God takes the souls of the righteous, for whom death does not need to be a form of atonement. It is the way that all people will die in *Yemos HaMoshiach*.

As promised, war will be an evil of the past. Amalek, and everything Amalekian, will also belong to the past, allowing for the fulfillment of the verse:

> On that day, God will be one and His Name, one. (*Zechariah* 14:9)

As *Rashi* explains at the end of *Parashas Beshallach* (*Shemos* 17:16), Amalek "divides" the Name of God into two parts: *Yud-Heh* and *Vav-Heh*. This means, in everyday terms, that he causes results that make men question the reality of God, and His involvement in the affairs of man.

The Torah says:

> You saw [the events of Mt. Sinai] in order to know that Hashem is Elokim, and there is nothing else besides Him. (*Devarim* 4:35)

This is the sum total of all that a Jew is supposed to believe with all of his heart. Amalek comes to confuse us, to create doubt in our minds as to the extent that God is involved in our everyday affairs. Hence, the *gematria* of his name—240—is the same as the Hebrew word for "doubt", *suffek*.

Everything that we do is for the sake of unifying the Divine Name, whether we are saying the "*Shema*", performing a basic *mitzvah*, or just taking time for ourselves. And, nothing does this more than acting in such a way that shows one's trust and faith in God, something that is not always so easy to do in this world.

However, in *Yemos HaMoshiach*, the struggle will be over. At that time of intense Divine revelation, Divine Providence will no longer be theoretical, on any level, but perfectly apparent in every aspect of Creation. This is what the Midrash means when it says:

> At this time, if a man goes out to collect figs on *Shabbos*, the figs say nothing. However, in the future, if a man collects figs on *Shabbos*, the figs will yell at him, *"Shabbos!"* (*Midrash Shochar Tov, Mizmor* 73)

We will probably have to wait until that time to see exactly what this *midrash* means. One thing is for certain: in *Yemos HaMoshiach*, the reality of God and His holy Torah will be all pervasive, making even accidental sins impossible. The clarity of the Divine Presence we enjoyed at Mt. Sinai will be even greater in *Yemos HaMoshiach*, making the experience of it already an aspect of the absolute pleasure we are destined to enjoy in *Olam HaBah*.

DAY THIRTY-THREE:
The Third Temple

Chazal, with their great wisdom and foresight, saw fit to establish the 9th day of Av as a national day of mourning over the loss of the temples, and a list of other terrible tragedies that occurred on that day throughout history. They knew that, after being in exile for so many centuries, the Jewish people would lose touch with the concept of a Jewish temple, especially after being exiled from their land for 2,000 years.

They were correct in their assessment, since even with *Tisha B'Av*, most Jews today have little appreciation of what it means to have the third and final temple arrive, whether by natural means, or through a Heavenly fire as the Talmud predicts. They don't give much thought to how having a temple will dramatically enhance the spiritual and physical quality of their lives.

The first thing a new temple means to the Jewish people is the return of the *Shechinah* to *Tzion*. Even though the Divine Presence will already have become tremendously enhanced, it will be more so after the temple is returned. No longer will foreign religions occupy anything in *Eretz Yisroel*, especially the Temple Mount.

When the gentiles return to Jerusalem to pray, it will be to the Jewish God, in a way that is acceptable to Torah, and with complete respect for the Jewish people. They will bring sacrifices and gifts for the temple and the Jewish people, because of their intense desire to join with the Jewish nation in their worship of God.

It will be commonplace for Jews to travel to Jerusalem, to see the temple and watch the *kohanim* perform their service once again. Today, if Jews travel to the *Kosel HaMa'aravi*—the Western Wall—on occasion, it is usually to catch a *minyan*, or to say some *tehillim*, and then leave.

As a person leaves the *Kosel*, and looks back, he sees a big stone wall, at the base of which are others still praying, while over the wall, he sees Arab mosques dominating the skyline. As moving an experience as going to the *Kosel* may be today, it becomes bitter-sweet when we are forced to recall how little control we have over the holiest site in the world.

However, in *Yemos HaMoshiach*, after the temple has returned, as a Jew ascends the stairs away from the Western Wall Court, and he looks back, he will see others Jews ascending to the Temple Mount area, with the proper amount of purity, and with no resistance. As he looks up, he will see the temple towering high above, completely dominating the view. He will see smoke arising straight up, as new sacrifices are offered up, as per the instructions of the Torah.

And, we will feel different. It won't have just been a great spiritual experience, it will have been a tangible interaction with the Creator of the Universe. The sense of spiritual lift will be greater than any other we have experienced during our present time. We will become in touch with our own sense of eternity, and it will be ultimately exhilarating.

This is certainly something to contemplate, and to yearn for.

Av 8

DAY THIRTY-FOUR:
Kohen, Levi, and Yisroel

Today, there is very little that distinguishes a *Kohen* from a *Levi*, and the two of them from a *Yisroel*, except, perhaps, when it comes to giving out *aliyos* in synagogue, or attendance at a funeral. There are some other laws today that do apply only to *Kohanim*, but for the most part, people don't even know what they are.

As a result, it makes little difference where a Kohen or Levi lives, or what they do for a living. As a result, it makes little difference where they shop for their food: if the food is sufficiently *kosher*, that is all that counts today.

In *Yemos HaMoshiach*, especially after the return of the temple, all of this will make a difference once again. Most of the *Kohanim* will move to Jerusalem, and live as close to the temple as possible. They won't need to own property, or earn a living, since they will once again be supported by the rest of the nation, as they resume their responsibility of the temple service on behalf of the entire Jewish people.

Likewise, the *Levi'im*, more than likely, will also take up residence close to the temple grounds, to be ready and available to resume their role in the temple service. They, too, like the *Kohanim*, will receive support from the tithes of the rest of the nation, so that they can focus on their spiritual responsibilities.

As for the rest of the people, they will see the miracles that result from the holy cycle of which they are a part. By supporting the temple service, the *Kohanim* are able to act as a conduit for the blessing God sends our way, and that blessing falls on the rest of the nation.

In the meantime, *Moshiach*, whose soul will be that of Moshe *Rabbeinu*—

> Moshe was the first redeemer, and he will be the final one as well, as it says in *Tikunim*, *Tikun* 69, 131a, and the *GR"A* there, on 137b. (*Hakdamos v'Sha'arim*, 6:1)

—but, who will have descended from Dovid *HaMelech*, will preside over the Jewish people as their *nasi*—prince— as did Moshe *Rabbeinu* in his own time.

No longer will there be any confusion about Torah or regarding any law. By that time, prophecy will already start returning to the entire Jewish nation, and we'll know a level of clarity that even the Generation of the Desert didn't know. They still had a *yetzer hara*; ours will be gone.

As a result, free-choice will have ended: no evil, no free-will. Which begs the question, what will life be about at that time? What will there be to do, if choosing to be moral is no longer a choice but the only way of life, as life becomes increasingly more miraculous, and the vision of God, increasingly more intense?

The answer is wonderful, and one worth yearning for: *tikun*. But, not the kind of *tikun* that comes through hard work, or as a result of suffering. It will be the kind of *tikun* to our bodies and souls that results from the warmth and glow of the light of God; just the revelation of God alone will be enough to rectify us, as part of the preparation for the World-to-Come.

Once *Moshiach* comes, and evil has been completely eradicated, then the light of God can increase daily for everyone, and the pleasure of receiving it will be tremendous, and just get better each day. The world will still be quite physical, but it certainly will feel incredibly spiritual, and forever uplifting.

Sadness, depression, and all such unfortunate states of mind will never exist again.

L'iluy Nishmat

Chayim Leib ben Shmuel HaLevi, z"l
Aharon ben Simcha Tiyhu Nafshoteyhem , z"l

Estner, Horvitz, and Baumoehl
Families

Av 9

DAY THIRTY-FIVE:
The Ninth of Av

Even though the *Kohanim* and *Levi'im* officiated in the *Mishkan* throughout the time in the desert, it was not the ideal circumstance. It had been a unique situation in which the close proximity of the *Shechinah* had elevated the camp of the Jewish nation, giving it a holier status than any other place in the Diaspora.

Even still, the *Mishkan* had not functioned on the same level that the future temple would. For the desert, it was an ideal situation. With respect to the ultimate goals of Creation and the Jewish people, it was far from it. So, when the Generation of the Spies refused to accept the gift of *Eretz Yisroel*, they had rejected more than just the land; they had rejected everything they had been redeemed from Egypt to become, as embodied in the temple that was destined to be built.

Hence, the intrinsic connection between the disaster of the Spies, and all of those destined to result on the *Tisha B'Avs* of the future:

"The entire assembly raised up and issued its voice; the people wept that night" (Bamidbar 14:1). Rabbah said in the name of Rebi Yochanan, "That night was the night of *Tisha B'Av*, and The Holy One, Blessed is He, told them, 'You cry

for nothing? I will establish a crying for the generations!'."
(Ta'anis 29a)

Hence, was born *Tisha B'Av*, a day of national mourning for the Jewish people. However, what it is really meant to be is a day of national yearning for the Jewish people, yearning for the temple and the Divine Presence meant to dwell within it, yearning for the return to the temple service of the *Kohanim* and *Levi'im*, yearning to live on the land in order to bear witness to all of this, and to participate in it.

Eventually, those who survived the 40 years in the desert entered the land, as God had promised:

> *Your young children of whom you said they will be taken captive, I will bring them; they will know the land that you have despised. (Bamidbar 14:31)*

They fought against the Canaanites, and took the land. Eventually, Shlomo *HaMelech* built the first temple in 2928/833 BCE, and it stood for 410 years, before being destroyed by Nebuchadnetzar in the year 3338/423 BCE. Exiled to Bavel, once again, the Jewish people found themselves outside the Land of Israel.

The Babylonian Exile lasted 70 years, 52 years under the rulership of Babylonian kings, and 18 years under that of Median kings, just as the Torah had predicted. Then it came time to return home, and to re-build what was supposed to have been the second and final temple. The miraculous victory of the Jewish people over Haman in 3407/353 BCE, was meant to initiate that process.

The Babylonian Exile should have been the last one, but it wasn't, and the question is, *why*?

Dedicated as a *z'chus* for our family and *K'lal Yisrael*.

Aharon Levi and Chaya Miriam Proctor
and family

Av 10

DAY THIRTY-SIX:
Wellsprings of Light

When many in the Torah world hear the word *"Kabbalah"*, or *"Sod"*, they feel as if they are trespassing on private property. It doesn't help that many people today learn Kabbalah, or aspects of it, even though they are totally unqualified to do so, creating quite a controversy.

However, sometimes it is important to draw from such knowledge to understand the answers to even basic questions. Not everyone wants to know how the body works in detail, but if someone becomes ill, *God forbid*, such knowledge can save his life.

Likewise, when things go wrong in history, it helps to have a deeper understanding of what was going on "behind the scenes", to better appreciate how to avoid such mistakes in the future. If you want to cure the symptoms, you have to first deal with their cause.

Most of us, when celebrating Purim, think only about the miraculous victory that brought down Haman and ended his diabolical plan to annihilate the Jewish people of his time. As a result, we focus only on the celebration aspect of the holiday, and do not contemplate the lesson it is also supposed to teach future generations, just as we do at the Pesach *Seder* each year as well (see *Day 20*).

However, the *Zohar* provides a very important insight as to why the Purim redemption was not the final one, as it ought to have been:

> Since the power of the kingdom of Bavel was removed, the "Lower *Heh*" [of God's four-letter Name] began to emanate light. However, since the Jewish people did not return to become purified from their impurity, to become the treasured nation as before, only a few at a time and as a mixture, and since they were not found in completion, the light of the "Upper *Yud*" [of God's Name and corresponding to the *sefirah* of *Chochmah*] did not descend that much as before, and therefore, the upper springs did not flow or give off light as before … (*Zohar, Shemos* 9b)

In simpler terms, the Purim redemption represented a very significant turning point in Jewish history. At that time, after the fall of Bavel, the upper spiritual realms were prepared to shower down Divine Light onto the Jewish people, making possible a temple on the level of the first one. This would have completely rectified the Jewish people, and for that matter, the entire world, ushering in the Messianic Era.

However, it didn't happen, for one reason only: not all the Jews came back from Bavel, choosing instead to stay in the Diaspora, even though they had permission to return to *Eretz Yisroel* and re-build the temple and the nation. As a result, the *Zohar* reveals, the holy light destined to be revealed at that time remained hidden above. Instead, future exiles remained in store for the Jewish people, and darkness descended upon the land.

The returning Jews from *Golus Bavel* had the opportunity to rectify the sin of the Spies, but failed a second time.

The rest, as they say, is history. And now, it is our history, since we are the most recent generation to live out the exile that should have ended back in the time of Mordechai and Esther. Knowing this may not make one want to pack up and move to the Holy Land, but at the very least, it ought to make one yearn to be able to yearn to do so.

Dedicated by the Apisdorf Family
for the *refuah shlaimah* **of**

Hershel Avraham ben Bracha
Yisroel Noach ben Hinda
Nachman ben Chana

Av 11

DAY THIRTY-SEVEN:
To Be A Zealot, Part 1

Imagine deciding to go away for Shabbos to some place relaxing, which is exactly the opposite of where your children want to spend their Shabbos.

"Do we have to go?" one child whines.
"It's so boring there!" another ones throws in.
"I'm not going!" declares the third one.

Even though you expected such a reaction, it is still somewhat upsetting to hear it. How do you respond, if your heart is set on heading out there for a long-earned break? It depends upon a few factors, including the day on which all of this is taking place.

If it is only Tuesday, it is easier to remain calm, and say:

"We're going, and you'll see that it is more enjoyable than you think, so stop complaining."

It probably won't matter to you that they are still complaining as you walk away, planning what to take with you on your Shabbos vacation. Being only Tuesday, there are still three days to get the children on side.

However, should Friday roll around, and as you load up the car to go, they are still resisting and putting up a fight, it becomes increasingly more difficult to suffer their complaints. Suddenly, as time slips away and Shabbos comes closer, you find yourself pulling rank and using threats to get everyone on board so that you can get going in good time.

When the Spies came back with their evil report and rejected *aliyah*, it was "Tuesday", so-to-speak. One might have expected God to say to them,

> "Look, the reason why you are not crossing the Jordan river today is because you are not ready to do so. You asked to spy the land; I didn't send you. In the meantime, stop complaining and wait and see. By the time you get to the border of *Eretz Canaan*, you'll be ready to cross it and all will go well, just as it did when you miraculously left Egypt and miraculously crossed the sea. Have a little trust already!"

However, instead God punished the Jewish people as if it was already "Friday", as if they were supposed to go in at that time, but had refused to do so. The question is, why was their rejection of *Eretz Yisroel* taken so sternly at a time that they weren't even required to enter the land yet? Why didn't God just tell them to wait a few days and see what changes were in store, what growth they were destined to accomplish in the meantime to prepare them for conquering the land?

Dedicated in memory of our dear father,

Rabbi Zev Segal, zt"l

A man who understood the meaning of saying little,
but doing a lot, and who, as a result of his devotion to Hashem
and his people, worked wonders and saved countless
spiritual lives.

Yigal Segal and Family

Av 12

DAY THIRTY-EIGHT:
To Be A Zealot, Part 2

To answer the question from the previous lesson, let's use another analogy.

Let's say you bought a gift for someone, and you want to know if it is truly what they want. If you simply give it to them, you know they will graciously accept it as if it is the most important gift in the world. They won't let you know if you made a mistake, because they value your friendship too much.

So, instead, you buy what you think is the perfect gift, and before wrapping it, you put it on your desk and invite your friend over. Leaving it in plain view, your friend enters your office, and right on cue, he notices the gift, and not knowing that it is for him, says, "Wow, this is great! I would love to have one of these!" at which point you smile from ear-to-ear, and tell him, "Good, because I bought it for you!"

In the same way, had the Jewish people shown up at the border of *Eretz Yisroel* on the day they were meant to enter it, it would have been a *mitzvah* to cross the Jordan river and take the land. Even if you enjoy doing a particular *mitzvah*, it is still something you have to do, because transgressing it has severe consequences.

However, had the Spies come back with the kind of enthusiasm that Kaleiv and Yehoshua had shown, it would have proven how much the Jewish people sincerely wanted the "gift" that *Eretz Yisroel* was meant to be (*Brochos* 5a). It would have shown God how much they appreciated all that the land embodied, and what living there means to enhancing once relationship with God and Torah.

To be a zealot, means to go the extra distance for a cause, even if it doesn't seem to be required, and sometimes, even at personal risk. And, when that cause is important to God, it is one of the most beautiful expressions of love and devotion to Him, and therefore, it is very dear to Him.

From the Jews who merited to enter the land and live there, only to be exiled 850 years later, we learn how important it is to appreciate living on the land. Until the time of exile, we had it good: a land, a temple, and God watching over us. Taking all of that for granted, we squandered it, and were forced into bitter exile for millennia to follow. And, it's not over yet.

From the Spies, and the Jews of Bavel who failed to return to *Eretz Yisroel* with the minority of the nation that did, we learn just how important it is to value the land even before it becomes a *mitzvah* to live there. We learn how important a spiritual opportunity it is to show God how much we love that which He values, especially at times when it is easy not to do so.

To be a Jew, is to be a zealot, whether it means going the extra distance for a simple *chesed*, performing a daily *mitzvah* with a little extra intention, or yearning for redemption at a time when others do not.

DAY THIRTY-NINE:
It's All In The Preparation

There is an interesting dialogue in the Talmud that is good advice for everyone. Apparently, it takes place in the future, after history as we know has come to an end, and it goes like this:

> The nations will plead, "Offer us the Torah anew and we shall obey it." However, The Holy One, Blessed is He, will tell them, "Foolish ones! He who took the trouble [to prepare] on *Erev Shabbos* can eat on Shabbos, but he who did not prepare on *Erev Shabbos*, what will he eat on Shabbos?" (*Avodah Zarah* 3a)

The meaning is simple: if you don't make the effort to prepare when you can, there will come a time when you'll wish you had, but won't be able to any longer. Times of crisis are not the time to learn anything, they are times to put into practice what you hopefully already know. How many crises have ended tragically because the people involved were unqualified to save the day?

The Talmud, elsewhere, teaches a similar lesson:

> A person doesn't sin unless a spirit of insanity enters him. (*Sotah* 3a)

That's good news, because an insane person is not held responsible for his sins. However, if only insane people sin, then why do we have Yom Kippur? Why is there even a threat of punishment for transgressing the Torah? No one should ever be culpable enough to be judged worthy of such punishment!

What the Talmud means is that when it comes to a moment of temptation, if a person is not prepared for it, then he becomes temporarily insane as his emotions and desires take control. It's like being on a strict diet, only to come to a food tasting contest, ravenous. What chance does a person have in such a test?

On the other hand, if a person anticipates a situation of temptation, and prepares himself against it, it can become a simple matter of passing the test with flying colors. When it comes to any kind of test, success depends upon advance preparation, as it says, "Who is the wise man? He who sees what is being born" (Tamid 32a), and prepares accordingly.

So, though it may be true that only people who are out of touch with reality sin, the real sin is in not preparing oneself in advance of the crisis. At such times, we are completely sane, and perfectly capable of rising to the occasion to prepare ourselves, so that when the moment of temptation arrives, we are well-fortified against it.

In a sense, this is what yearning for the Final Redemption, and for Eretz Yisroel represents. It is our preparation in advance of the event itself, may it happen in our time. It shows God that, when the moment comes, and it can come at the blink of an eye, we want to be as ready as possible, so as to not make any mistakes in terms of response. And, when Heaven sees how prepared we are to prepare ourselves, they make a point of making sure that we are as successful as we prepared to be.

Dedicated by Yitzi & Sara Lefkowitz

To all our friends who have made *aliyah* and make
our life so rich here in Israel.

And, to all our friends who need to make *aliyah* but
haven't realized it yet. Hashem Misses You!
Come Home.

Av 14

DAY FORTY:
Maximize Your Time

It sounds somewhat presumptuous: How do you prepare for the Final Redemption? Who says you even have to prepare? Why not just wait to see what happens, when it happens?

Because, when it comes to Jewish history, that has rarely been a good idea. It is not a contradiction of *bitachon* and *emunah*—trust and faith in God—to prepare oneself in the event that redemption takes place in one's lifetime. It's really part of the fulfillment of anticipating the possible arrival of *Moshiach* any day, especially when you consider the following:

> Rav Elchanan [Wasserman] concluded that one must suffer the pangs of *Moshiach*, but the wise man will quietly prepare himself during that time ... perhaps he will be worthy of seeing the comforting of *Tzion* and *Yerushalayim*. (*Leiv Eliyahu, Shemos*, page 172)

Hopefully, the "pangs of *Moshiach*" won't be so bad for us, but avoiding them may depend upon our preparation. The more real we are with the concept of redemption, the less real God will have to make it to us. So, then, how does one prepare for such a major historical event?

To begin with, take time more seriously. Spiritually seriously. We take for granted our most important asset and commodity: free-will. We are here in this world specifically to use our free-will to earn merit to maximize our portion in the World-to-Come (*Derech Hashem*, 1:2:1-1:3:2). It is easy to forget this on a daily basis, since life is so distracting with its mundane, temporal matters.

However, once the Final Redemption is complete, the period of free-will comes to an end, and we will lose the age-old opportunity to earn additional reward for the World-to-Come. This will probably come as a shock to a lot of people who barely ever thought about using, let alone losing, their power of choice. It probably won't be too uncommon to hear people moaning, *"If only I had known ... I would have made more good choices!"*

How much more so will this be the case when we find out what good choices are worth in terms of the World-to-Come, and what bad choices take away from it. This is something worth thinking about on a daily basis, as the rabbis taught:

> Consider the loss incurred for performing a *mitzvah* compared to its reward, and the benefit received for sinning compared to the loss. (*Pirkei Avos* 2:1)

The Talmud says that one of the gravest sins is *bitul Torah*—using time that could have been spent learning Torah to do less important things (*Brochos* 5a). It doesn't just mean wasting learning time, but wasting time by doing something less meaningful than the moment might have allowed. To be real with redemption is to be real with time, and there is no better opportunity to be real with time than the present.

Av 15

DAY FORTY-ONE:
Learn *Nevi'im*

It is incredible how unimportant *Nevi'im*—the Prophets—has become over the generations. We're not talking about *Mishlei*, or *Koheles*, which, though they may have been written with *Ruach HaKodesh*, are not prophecy. We're talking about *Nevi'im*, which is completely prophecy, the word of God delivered to man through confirmed prophets.

Yet, so few people learn it today, as if what it has to say only applied to past generations. People learn *Chumash*, because that is the source of the *mitzvos*. We learn *gemora*, because that is how we understand the correct way to perform the *mitzvos* in all their glorious detail. We learn the *Rishonim* and *Acharonim*, to make sure that we learned the *gemora* correctly, and to advance our own learning skills. And, we have probably added some *mussar* and *hashkofah*, just to round out our learning program.

But no *Navi*, or very little of it, which is really remarkable when you consider that their prophecies, written down about two millennia ago, are for us. We could not merit to have prophecy in our time, so God did the next best thing: He had the prophets of their time speak about our time, so that we could benefit from prophecy even though we don't have prophets.

True, some of the prophecies are quite frightening. However, whatever hasn't happened can still be avoided, but only if we know what to avoid. God gave us these prophecies so that we can recognize the meaning of what might otherwise be confusing events, allowing us to better respond to the spiritual needs of the moment, specifically to avoid disaster.

Learning *Navi* is like putting on glasses to enhance one's vision. A person with poor vision can often make things out, but not clearly. He can, somewhat, guess what he is looking at, but he can't see any pertinent details. As a result, he can be mistaken about what he thinks he sees. Or, worse, he may not see it at all, which can certainly be dangerous.

Lots of events are occurring today, and it is hard to tell how significant they are, at least in terms of the "big picture" of Jewish history. One day, it will all be clear. In the future, looking back on today, the people living at that time will be able to see what were turning points in our time, and were not. However, that doesn't help those of us living through these crucial times.

Learning *Nevi'im* does. The more one learns *Navi*, the more one can look at current history with a discerning eye, and make decisions that can actually mean life-or-death. God gave us *Nevi'im* so that we could see the events of our time in the proper Torah and historical context, so why disregard that gift? Why ignore such an advantage?

Yearning for redemption depends upon it.

Av 16

DAY FORTY-TWO:
A Holy Mindset

The Jewish people are on a mission, and it can be summed up in two words: *Kiddush Hashem*, to sanctify the Name of God. This is not just something we do on the side, but something that is supposed to result from everything we do, whether alone or in public.

> Rav Papa asked Abaye: "Why is it that for the former generations miracles were performed and for us miracles are not performed? It cannot be because of their learning, because in the years of Rav Yehudah, their learning was confined to *Nezikin*, and we learn all six orders ... And yet, when Rav Yehudah took off one shoe [during a drought on a fast day], rain used to come. We torment ourselves and cry loudly, and no one pays attention to us!" He answered: "The former generations used to sacrifice themselves for *Kiddush Hashem*; we do not sacrifice ourselves for *Kiddush Hashem*." (*Brochos* 20a)

What does it mean to sanctify the Name of God? There are many ways to do it, but they all result in the same thing: more of God's Presence in Creation. The opposite term, "*Chillul Hashem*", the profanation of God's Name, comes from the word "*challal*", which means a "void". Something that profanes God's Name has the impact of making Creation somewhat void of the Presence of God, the extent to which depends upon the severity of the *Chillul Hashem*.

Kiddush Hashem has the opposite effect, by drawing more Divine light into Creation, thereby making the Presence of God more pronounced. That's why a *Kiddush Hashem* can occur even when a person is alone, and no one else is around to witness it; it will still impact Creation in a positive way.

The longer the Jewish people remain in exile, the more we begin to mimic the host nations amongst whom we live, blurring the distinction between Jew and gentile. Eventually, our actions, even as Torah Jews, may fall into the category of those which are acceptable by world standards, but not by Torah standards, resulting in a *Chillul Hashem*, and sometimes, severe ones.

This is very dangerous for everyone. Reducing the *Shechinah* in Creation, *l'havdil*, is like not keeping up sanitary conditions in a hospital: unhealthy stuff fills the void, endangering the lives of everyone. The more Creation becomes void of the Presence of God, the more spiritual impurity fills the void, corrupting man and Creation, a situation that Heaven will put up with for only so long. We've seen what results when we cross that line.

As the *gemora* says, doing that which sanctifies the Name of God brings special Divine Providence, anything from success in business to good relationships, to, perhaps, personal salvation from a life-threatening circumstance. Aside from being a Torah *mitzvah*, it is a wise step in the direction of the Final Redemption.

Av 17

DAY FORTY-THREE:
Shabbos and Redemption

One of the first *mitzvos* the Jewish people received after leaving Egypt was that of Shabbos. As the Midrash explains, they had already been resting on the seventh day of the week, even while still enslaved in Egypt, thanks to the advice of Moshe *Rabbeinu* to Pharaoh. However, in Marah, Shabbos became *halachah* (*Sanhedrin* 56b).

Shabbos is considered to be the cornerstone of Judaism, since it embodies so much of what Torah is all about. Therefore, by keeping its laws, as a nation, we merit to see everyday life transformed into a permanent state of Shabbos:

> Rebi Yochanan said in the name of Rebi Shimon bar Yochai: "If the Jewish people were to keep two *Shabboses* according to the law, they would be redeemed immediately." (*Shabbos* 118b)

This is because the proper observance of Shabbos results in a state of redemption—every Shabbos. For the time being, until the rest of the nation gets with the program and observes Shabbos properly, the redemptive power of Shabbos remains an opportunity for individuals only. When

Shabbos is observed both in law and spirit, it is a great way to prepare for redemption.

Hence, the *gemora* adds:

> Rebi Shimon ben Pazzi said in the name of Rebi Yehoshua ben Levi, in Bar Kappara's name: One who eats three meals on Shabbos is saved from three evils: *Chevlei Moshiach*, the judgment of *Gihenom*, and the war of Gog and Magog. (*Shabbos* 118a)

These are three catastrophic events that all of us would like to avoid, at just about any cost. Why would the three Shabbos meals, a *mitzvah* that is *very* easy to perform, be the reason to be spared from any of them? What is so redeeming about fulfilling the *halachah* of three Shabbos meals? The reward seems to be far out of proportion to the effort made to receive it.

The *Maharal* explains:

> The three meals teach about the good that is in Creation of God. Therefore, these three meals, which represent the good and perfection within Creation, save from three punishments that represent what is missing within Creation. (*Chidushei Aggados, Shabbos* 118a)

In other words, Shabbos represents the perfection of Creation, and the pleasure that comes from eating the three meals is meant to be a way to experience that good. By eating them, and ideally, with this intention, one becomes part of that perfection, and is influenced by it, saving him from punishments that come because of what goes wrong in Creation. Hence, it is very important to eat all three meals, and with this intention.

However, there is another aspect to Shabbos that is very important, because it actually represents the transition from this stage of history to the next one, that of *Yemos HaMoshiach*. It's what went wrong in the desert, and that which we have been trying to rectify ever since.

This *shiur* is dedicated to the most revered memory of

Ya'akov Yehudah Goldfinger, z"l

our dear *mechutin*, and the grandfather, and great-grandfather of our mutual grandchildren.

A true *"Ish Chesed,"* he was the patriarch of the Goldfinger and Fishbein families, devoted to doing good deeds. And, he was a Holocaust survivor who was fortunate to establish a family, together with his dear wife, Devorah, z"l. He will be remembered lovingly by all.

The Neumark Family

Av 18

DAY FORTY-FOUR:
The True Double Portion

When the Jews left Egypt, they ate *matzah* for the next 30 days, until it ran out. Just in advance of this, they complained to Moshe *Rabbeinu* about a lack of bread, at which point, God introduced them to the concept of the *munn*—Heavenly bread.

As the Torah reports, every individual was supposed to collect one *omer*, about 2 quarts, of *munn* each day. If they collected too little, it became an *omer* in their vessel; if they collected too much, the surplus rotted, as did any *munn* that was left over until the morning. The rule was, one *omer* of *munn* per person per day, to be consumed before the next morning.

The only exception was *Erev Shabbos*, as the Torah states:

> On the sixth day, they must prepare that which they bring in, which will be twice as much as they usually collect. (*Shemos* 16:5)

Unfortunately, by the time *Erev Shabbos* came around, Moshe had yet to tell them about the double portion. Instead, the Torah reports that they learned it on their own, and much to their surprise:

On the sixth day, however, they collected a double portion, two omers per person, and all the princes of the congregation came and told Moshe. He said to them, "This is what God said ..." (Shemos 16:22-23)

On the surface of it, nothing is unusual. However, the verse in which God tells Moshe to explain to the Jewish people that they would be able to collect two *omers Erev Shabbos*, begins with the word *"v'hayah"* (*Shemos* 16:5), which the *gemora* says is the "language of *smichah*", foreshadowing a positive event about to occur (*Megillah* 10b). However, the verse in which the Jewish people discover the miracle of the second *omer* begins with the word *"v'yehi"*, which the *gemora* says is the "language of trouble", foreshadowing a negative event that is about to occur.

What negative event occurred? On the contrary, discovering the bonus *omer* for themselves was probably more exciting than being told about it in advance. If anything, that verse should begin with *"v'hayah"*, to indicate the surprise and joy the Jewish people must have felt at the time.

This is the answer:

This was the joy of the sixth day, that speech alone was enough to prepare and designate a different bread for Shabbos: different in measure, different in smell and taste, and different in appearance. It did not require any additional effort or act. For this reason, when Moshe was told to command them regarding the preparation for Shabbos, it was said in the language of joy: *"V'hayah b'yom hashishi ..."* since, a minute effort of speech was enough to complete the bread that was different. However, Moshe did not tell them the matter of *"On the sixth day they shall prepare ..."* until after they came and inquired about it ... For this reason, the Torah punishes him as well when it says, *"For how long will you not believe in Me?"* (*Shemos* 16:28), including Moshe in the criticism, as *Rashi* says. If so, then, at the time they went out to collect the *munn* on *Erev Shabbos*, they had yet to learn the matter of the joy of *Erev Shabbos*, that speech alone is enough to prepare and designate the bread to be different for Shabbos. Therefore, they went out thinking that they would have to actually collect a double portion of the *omer* for each person, having assumed already that the sixth day had to be different from the previous five days ... (*Ze'ev Yitraf, Ze'ev HaKohen Hoberman, "Krias Shabbos Oneg"*)

And, what were they supposed to have said?

This is a source from a verse for what the *Magen Avraham* brings (250:1), that a person is supposed to say regarding everything he buys, *"This is for the honor of Shabbos."* The *Mishnah Brurah* adds that speech helps to increase the holiness. (Ibid.)

In other words, had Moshe *Rabbeinu* taught the matter to the Jewish people in advance of their going out and collecting the *munn Erev Shabbos*, he would have told them, "Before you pick up the *omer*, say, 'This is for the honor of Shabbos', and the *omer* will become two *omers* on its own, for the sake of Shabbos." However, instead, they actually collected two *omers* for each person, and the miracle was only that the second *omer* didn't dissolve as it did the rest of the week.

Understanding the difference between the two approaches is critical for preparing for the Final Redemption and *Yemos HaMoshiach*.

Av 19

DAY FORTY-FIVE:
Supernatural Channels

The difference between the two approaches is very distinct: it is a much greater miracle and source of joy to watch one *omer* of *munn* miraculously become two *omers*. For two *omers* of *munn* to not become one may also be miraculous, but it is also the kind of miracle for which the scientific world as a name: phenomenon. The event, according to all known rules, should not have occurred, but you can't deny reality. You can only analyze it to understand the new rule the phenomenon teaches.

What was the message that the *munn* of *Erev Shabbos* was supposed to teach the Jewish people? That material success, for the Jew, ideally, should come through spiritual channels. For, the journey through the desert was all for the sake of preparing the Jewish people for living in *Eretz Yisroel*, and this lesson of the *munn* was the very underpinning of daily life in *Eretz Yisroel*, a place where material success comes through spiritual channels:

> The land you are about to possess is not like Egypt from where you came, and in which, if you sowed seeds, you had to bring water to them as you would for a garden of green herbs. The land you are about to possess has mountains and deep valleys, and is watered by rain from the sky—a land which God, your God, cares for, God, your God pays atten-

tion to continuously the entire year. (*Devarim* 11:11-12)

It is a lesson about life that we struggle with to this very day. And, to make sure the point was not lost forever, it was repeated in the incident with the rock that Moshe was told to speak to in order to bring forth water for the thirsty Jewish nation (*Bamidbar* 20:1). At the end of the 40 years in the desert, poised to enter *Eretz Yisroel*, it was crucial to learn the lesson of "*Yaish m'Ayin*".

Yaish M'Ayin, or "something from nothing", is usually the term used to describe a crucial aspect of the Creation process. Historically, there was a time when nothing physical existed anywhere, just the completely spiritual light of God. And then, God made Creation, which is quite physical. That critical moment of time that God's completely spiritual light created something physical is called "*Yaish m'Ayin*."

Of course, "nothing" is a relative term. To a physical being, it's as if the spiritual world doesn't even exist, even though it is more "real" than the physical world. We can't see it, touch it, smell it, or interact with it using any of our five, physical senses. That is not a limitation of the spiritual world, but of our five senses.

Physical solutions to physical problems begin in the spiritual realm. The Jewish people needed two portions of *munn* for Shabbos, which, as God had told Moshe, had already been set aside in the spiritual realm. This is what the *gemora* means when it says that, when it comes to the Jewish people, the remedy is prepared before the illness (*Megillah* 10b).

On *Erev Shabbos*, by saying the words, "*This is for the honor of Shabbos*" before collecting it, each Jew would have been able to draw that spiritual reality into the physical realm—on his own. The previous five days of the week, God did it for the nation.

Likewise, the first time Moshe *Rabbeinu* brought forth water from the rock, he struck it with his staff, a physical act. Even though it was a miracle, physical interaction to produce the water made it less so, more *yaish m'yaish*, something from something, so-to-speak. That time, it was only to provide water for a complaining, thirsty people.

However, the second time Moshe *Rabbeinu* brought forth water from the rock, it was to teach the Jewish people how blessing is accessed in *Eretz Yisroel*: *yaish m'Ayin*— directly from God, direct from the spiritual realm. By talking to the rock, a spiritual act, Moshe *Rabbeinu* was mimicking life in *Eretz Yisroel*.

Needless to say, just as the lesson was not taught through the *munn*, it was not taught through the incident with the rock either, forcing us to learn it the hard way, throughout history. Perhaps, our miraculous survival over the course of 3,319 very difficult years itself is meant to be the proof, that when it comes to the Jewish people, it is a matter of *yaish m'Ayin*—survival direct from the hand of God.

As the end of history approaches, you can expect to see life become a test, for the Jew, of belief in this concept. By anticipating it, and preparing for it, it will be a smoother transition, and a safer one, and a great source of merit in this world, and the next one.

Av 20

DAY FORTY-SIX:
Kotzer Ruach

The first time Moshe went down to Egypt to save the Jewish people, Pharaoh didn't listen to him, just as God had forewarned. However, to Moshe's surprise and consternation, making the demand, and instilling the Jewish people with hope of redemption, resulted in Pharaoh increasing the slavery to impossible levels.

Thus, the next time Moshe *Rabbeinu* came to redeem the Jewish nation, they were a broken people. The Hebrew term is, *"kotzer ruach"*, which *Rashi* explains to mean "shortness of breath" (*Shemos* 6:9). They were like people who could not catch their breath, let alone pay attention to Moshe *Rabbeinu's* second promise of redemption.

God runs the world, and everything in it. Yes, we have free-will, but up to a point. It is amazing how much good man can do, and, unfortunately, how much evil as well. However, the moment God decides enough is enough, everything becomes secondary to His will, and history will follow a specific course no matter how hard man tries to change it.

If so, then what was the purpose of having Moshe *Rabbeinu* go down to Egypt, demand the release of God's people, the descendants of Avraham, Yitzchak, and Ya'akov, and fail? At the time, was it not a tremendous

Chillul Hashem? Furthermore, why would God allow Moshe's attempt at salvation result in just the opposite: increased slavery?

The answer has to do with the overall goal of Creation, as God told Moshe *Rabbeinu*:

> God said to Moshe, "Come to Pharaoh. I have hardened his heart, and those of his servants, in order to perform My signs among them, so you can relate it to your son, and your son's son, how I mocked Egypt, and about the signs I performed among them, so you will know that I am God." (*Shemos* 10:1-2)

That is what it is all about: *knowing God*. Not just knowing *about* God, but about knowing God as much as is humanly possible. The goal is a knowledge of God that is so perfect that one is never fooled by anything within Creation that gives the appearance that it has power independent of God's. All power must be ascribed only to God.

> Hear O Israel, the Lord our God, the Lord is One. (*Devarim* 6:4)

> You saw [the events of Mt. Sinai] in order to know that Hashem is Elokim, and there is nothing else besides Him. (*Devarim* 4:35)

That's the way it was at the beginning, in the Garden of Eden, before the sin of the *Aitz HaDa'as Tov v'Rah*. That is the way it is going to be at the end, after *Moshiach* rids the world of evil, and the *yetzer hara* is no more. In-between, history has seen many tyrants rise up who have tried to usurp the power of God, or, at least make it appear that way in the minds of men, most notably, Amalek.

And, history has seen billions of people fall for the ruse, and pay for it as a result. This, apparently, is what necessitates *kotzer ruach*, a situation in which all false sources of hope no longer exist, so that we can ascribe our salvation only to God.

Dedicated in memory of

Yitzchak Issar ben Baruch, z"l

**As this book is striving to elevate the Jewish people,
may his Neshamah also have an elevation.**

Av 21

DAY FORTY-SEVEN:
With Perfect Clarity

For the redemption from Egypt to be a physical success, God could have had a simple, natural plague destroy Egyptian society, as He did to the army of Sancheriv during the siege of Jerusalem in Chizkiah *HaMelech's* time. After all, four-fifths of the Jewish people died in the Plague of Darkness anyhow, so what difference would it have made had they died from a plague instead?

However, for the redemption from Egypt to be a spiritual success, there had to be no doubt, at least in the minds of the Jewish people who finally went free with Moshe *Rabbeinu*, that God, and only God had saved them. The redemption from Egypt was not about freeing a broken and embittered nation, it was about building one whose entire existence is clearly dependent on its relationship with the Creator of the Universe.

Given the nature of man, for that to happen, every other means of escape and survival had to fail—completely. *Kotzer ruach* meant that the Jewish people had given up on every other "natural" form of redemption. After Moshe *Rabbeinu* failed to free them the first time, and after the slavery was increased as a result, they saw that they had no where to place their hope and trust in the physical world.

It was into this intellectual and emotional void that the light of God flowed, rejuvenating the broken Jewish nation, gradually rebuilding them spiritually and physically. Each plague, as it subsequently destroyed the Egyptian nation and its will, re-built the Jewish people, and their confidence. As a result, by the time the tenth plague of the death of the firstborn began, not one surviving Jew had any doubt whatsoever Who was responsible for their survival and salvation.

That is the way it will be at the end of history as we know it as well—

On that day, God will be one and His Name, one. (Zechariah 14:9)

—which means that the events leading up to the Final Redemption, as was in the case of Egypt, will promote such a perception. As in Egypt, over time, all false sources of security will probably fail, or disappear, until we have no one to rely upon except for our Father-in-Heaven.

At this stage of history, though many may already know this message, few have been able to integrate it. While our mouths may articulate the words, our actions and lifestyles may not quite be expressions of such a belief, since many are overly dependent upon secondary sources of survival, at the cost of relying solely on the Primary Source Himself.

Preparing for the Final Redemption is about becoming real with this concept. It is about developing as clear an understanding and appreciation of what it means and its importance now, so that when God perfects that clarity through the events of history, we'll have done most of the work on our own, already.

Av 22

DAY FORTY-EIGHT:
Makers and Pawns

History is divided between two types of people, makers and pawns. Makers are the kinds of people who take up causes, to make things better or worst. The ones who make things better are righteous in God's eyes, partners with Him in Creation. The ones who choose to make things worst are evil, and have no share in God's Creation, present or future.

Then there are the pawns, the vast majority of people throughout history who simply minded their own business whenever they could. Rather than impact history, they are usually impacted by it, often the "victims" of other people's schemes and plans. Nothing is by accident (*Chullin* 7b), and everything is the will of God, but if someone chooses to play the part of a pawn, then that is the role God allows him to play.

No question, it is easier to be a pawn. If history is peaceful, one can get away with simply taking as much responsibility for the fulfillment of Creation as is necessary to fulfill his own personal life. However, reward in the World-to-Come will also be limited, because, as the rabbis teach, "According to the effort is the reward" (*Pirkei Avos* 5:26). And, no effort earns greater reward in the World-to-Come as the ones made on behalf of the nation as a whole.

God gave some of His glory to man, so that he can be a partner with Him in Creation, building Heaven and its upper realms through all of his actions and deeds that he performs in this world. (*Sha'arei Leshem*, p. 76)

There is no question that every *mitzvah* performed brings great reward in the World-to-Come. We can't even begin to imagine how much. There is no question that, when a person performs a *chesed*, Heaven smiles. And, as the *Nefesh HaChaim* emphasizes in the fourth section, the learning of Torah maintains Creation.

Nevertheless, there is no better way to prepare for the Final Redemption than by playing a role in it. What kind of role? It depends upon the person, the opportunity, the time of history, and the will to get involved. It may be something as basic as saying one chapter of *Tehillim* each day, just for the sake of speeding up the redemption, or something as involving as starting an organization that furthers the cause itself.

The reward is tremendous for a variety of reasons. First of all, according to the *GR"A*, though God provides Heavenly help for every *mitzvah* we do, the help, when it comes to redemption-oriented activities, can be many times more than the effort we ourselves make. This means that we can succeed far beyond our expectations.

Furthermore, by being a partner in redemption, we put ourselves on the inside track. This means that, rather than simply being pawns in the process, we are makers of it, together with God and all the other people who consciously choose to play a role in redemption. Not only is this very rewarding, but it adds an element of safety for all those taking an active role in *Geulah Shlaimah*.

Av 23

DAY FORTY-NINE:
To Be A Maker

Even in the world of Makers, there are levels, because history, from a Torah perspective is not simple. It can't be. Otherwise, there wouldn't be enough challenge to make free-will meaningful, and accomplishments gratifying.

To be a real partner with God in the fulfillment of Creation, it helps to know how this world works, not just on a physical and obvious level, but behind the scenes. There are rules and objectives to Creation, some of which we are aware in the context of everyday life, others of which are hidden until someone makes a point of finding them.

And yet, they play a major role in life, and often provide important clues for understanding history and its opportunities. Some can take years to research and understand, but to the extent that a Jew makes that effort is to the extent that he can become a conscious partner with the Creator of the world in perfecting it.

For example, there is concept called *"mirmos v'tachboles"*, which literally translates as, "trickery and scheming". In this case, it is not talking about dishonest business people, but the way to bring about the Final Redemption without arousing the interest and resistance of the *Sitra Achra*.

We're always trying to outsmart the *Sitra Achra*, who at, first, plays the role of the *yetzer hara* to tempt us to sin. Then, after the sin, he becomes himself as he accuses us before the Heavenly Court, demanding justice against us. If he is successful in his case against us, then he becomes the punishing angel as well (*Bava Basra* 16a). For the *Sitra Achra*, it's all in a day's work, because that is what he was created to do: make free-will meaningful.

It makes life quite the game, except that this "game" has life and death consequences, if not physical ones, certainly spiritual ones. As the Talmud teaches, righteous people are alive even after they have died, and evil people are dead even while they still live (*Brochos* 18a).

There is a story about the *Chofetz Chaim* in his later years, how once, getting up early for *Shacharis* as had been his custom for decades, was approached by his *yetzer hara*, who said:

> "Old man, why are you up so early in the morning? After all these years, surely you deserve to sleep in and wake up later!"

To which the *Chofetz Chaim* responded:

> "If you're up this early in the morning, why shouldn't I be?"

Did the *Chofetz Chaim* really hear the voice of the *Sitra Achra*, his *yetzer hara*? Sure, as we all do, each time we are tempted to do that which we really ought not to, or each time we don't do that we should do. It's just that, for most of us, the voice of the *yetzer hara* sounds like our own, so we follow its advice as if it is our own advice.

After all, our *yetzer tov* and *yetzer hara* share the same brain—ours:

> Yoel called it (i.e., the *yetzer hara*) "*Tzafoni*"—Hidden One—as it says, "*I will distance Tzafoni from you ...*" (*Yoel* 2:20). Our rabbis taught: *I will distance Tzafoni from you*: this is the *yetzer hara* that is hidden and stands in the person's heart. (*Succah* 52a)

And, unless one knows how to distinguish one from the other, it is easy to confuse one for the other during a time of spiritual crisis. It is amazing how well people can rationalize the wrong, and transform it into right, and bad into good.

The *Chofetz Chaim*, being the great and righteous man that he was, was a master player of the *yetzer hara's* game. He knew his tricks, and therefore, knew how to out-trick him at his own game. The story is one of *mirmos v'tachboles*, first by his *yetzer hara*, who had a good case, and then, by the *Chofetz Chaim* himself, who had a better one, and therefore, was able to win the battle and do the *mitzvah*, once again, "*after all these years*".

It is a good analogy for all of us to follow, and it puts a person in charge of his own house, so-to-speak. It is a necessary piece of information if a person wants to move up from the level of Pawn to Maker. For, it is the *yetzer hara's* desire to do just the opposite, and not get involved in anything beyond that which gives us personal pleasure.

However, its ultimate application applies to something far greater than even an entire lifetime; it applies to all of Jewish history.

Av 24

DAY FIFTY:
Making Sense of It All

After years of pursuing God at a time that mankind was Godless, Avraham *Avinu* was rewarded with prophecy, and an eternal covenant for him and all of his descendants. And, keeping that covenant can be summed up by the words:

> When Avram was 99 years old, God appeared to Avram and He said to him, "I am God Almighty, walk before Me and be tamim." (*Bereishis* 17:1)

For the most part, the word "*tamim*" is translated as "perfect", something which, as *Rashi* explains, Avraham was about to become through *Bris Milah*. However, the word "*shalaim*", as used with respect to Ya'akov *Avinu* after his struggle with the angel (*Bereishis* 3:18), would have been more appropriate to express such an idea.

Therefore, "*tamim*" has an additional nuance of meaning: be simple in your perfection. Be up front with God and Torah. Man has a tendency to "serve" God in the most convoluted ways, rationalizing that which really ought not to be rationalized, all in the Name of God. Serve God in a straightforward manner, and you will never stray from this covenant.

Ironically, Jewish history has been anything but *tamim*. From its inception, perfection has been pursued through the least simplest of means, at least from man's perspective. The very creation of the dynasty of *Moshiach*, beginning with the birth of Avraham from idol-worshipping Terach, to the birth of the ancestor of Dovid *HaMelech* on one side from the union of Yehudah and his daughter-in-law, Tamar, and on the other side, from that of Lot and his daughter, to the rest of Jewish history, has been anything but straightforward! What has been going on?

Mirmos v'tachboles.

As mentioned before, *Yemos HaMoshiach* represents utopia for mankind, but annihilation for the *Sitra Achra*, *yetzer hara*, and *Malach HaMaves* (see *Lesson* 32). Therefore, as much as we long for history as we know it to come to a conclusion so that *Yemos HaMoshiach* can finally begin, the *Sitra Achra* wants it not to begin even more. Therefore, he will do anything he can to thwart it, or at least hold it off for as long as can.

In the end, he is still only doing his job, making redemption a matter of free-will, creating resistance that we have to choose to overcome in order to usher in the period of *Yemos HaMoshiach*. And, what's worse is that he does such a good job that people are either intimidated to get involved, or they have just lost interest in the topic altogether, distracted instead by everyday concerns and pleasures.

Nevertheless, regardless of what we do or how much we participate in the redemption process, it has to come; there are Heavenly deadliness that have to be met. We can choose to either bring them about on our terms, or let them come about on their own terms, which rarely works well for the Jewish people.

But who wants to engage the *Sitra Achra* head on? As the Talmud states, "Do not open your mouth to the *Satan*" (*Kesuvos* 8b), which means, don't start up with the *Sitra Achra*, because doing so can have disastrous results. How much more so is this true if one is attempting to bring out redemption, and therefore, the demise of the *Sitra Achra* himself?

Hence, explains the *Arizal*, there is the concept of *mirmos v'tachboles*. It is at the root of every major historical event meant to advance the cause of *Moshiach's* arrival, and which has occurred in a seemingly non-Torah way (*Sha'ar HaGilgulim*, Ch. 38).

"*What can be born from a man such as Terach?*" mocked the *Sitra Achra*, only to be shocked, when it was already too late, by the birth of Avraham *Avinu*. "*What can result from the union of a father and his daughter?*" he snickered, only to be thrown for a loop once the righteous Rus emerged, and became available for *yibum* with Boaz, the descendant of Yehudah and Tamar.

For, when it comes to *geulah*, you have to make it seem as if just the opposite is being accomplished as long as you possibly can. Otherwise, as the *GR"A* found out in his time, one encounters obstacles and roadblocks all the way, as the *Sitra Achra* fights to save his own skin, and cost us ours. The only way to make significant progress, explained the *Arizal*, is with the use of *mirmos v'tachboles*.

The only problem is that Heaven has done such a good job of it, that, unfortunately, even we have been fooled as well, perhaps even misjudging the redemption that is already well in progress.

Av 25

DAY FIFTY-ONE:
Make A Difference

In a world of about 6.6 billion people, it is hard to imagine making a difference to history. Even if we talk only about the Jewish nation, which has a population of about 12 million people worldwide, it is hard to imagine, for the average Jew, making a significant impact on the direction and success of the Jewish people as a whole.

However, often what stands between the Makers and the Pawns of history is not money, position, or power. It is usually two things: perception of a problem and the desire to do something about it. You can't fix something that you can't see is broken, and, you won't try to fix that which you think you can't fix.

A person who was planning a project to have a significant, and seemingly impossible, impact on the Jewish people was asked, "What do you expect to do? How do you expect to reach that many people, and, even if you reach them, how do you expect them to change their minds and get them to hear your message?"

Undaunted, he answered, "What difference does it make? What is the alternative, no project at all? If I do nothing, I will fail for sure. If I do something, even if I fail, I will know, at least, that I did my best to succeed. Don't forget that Pinchas required 12 miracles to make him successful against Zimri (*Bamidbar Rabbah* 20:26). In other words, naturally speaking, the odds were stacked against him, and yet, that didn't stop him, because win or lose, he had to choose, and he chose to make a difference. In fact, he'd rather die making a difference, than live and make none at all."

This is what the Talmud says:

> One who comes to purify himself, they help him … One who comes to sanctify himself, they sanctify him. (*Shabbos* 104a)

In other words, our responsibility is to make the effort, to take steps in the right direction, and leave the rest up to Heaven. We only have to make an opening the size of a pinhole, and Heaven will find a way to drive a wagon through it. In God's world, small efforts can have huge effects, when they are in the right direction and with the right intention.

As we learn from the Torah, crises, from a Divine perspective, are really spiritual opportunities. As chaotic as history can seem to become, it is never out of control, at least not out of God's control. Even in the worst circumstances, there remains an opportunity to rise to the occasion and make a difference on some level.

In the Torah, Pinchas merited to end the crisis in his time because he had developed himself into the kind of zealot who could perform the necessary deed. The daughters of Tzelofchad merited to teach an important law regarding inheritance of *Eretz Yisroel* because of their inherent love of the land, like their great ancestor before them (*Rashi, Bamidbar* 27:4).

If we plan to make a difference during the quiet times, then God will find a way to give us the opportunity to do so during the times of crisis.

Dedicated in loving memory of my mother,

Pesha Halpern,
Pesia bas R' Meir, z"l

(Yahrtzeit: 22 Elul 5759)

Dinah Lewitan

Av 26

DAY FIFTY-TWO:
Learn To See

The story of Pinchas ben Elazar ben Aharon *HaKohen* is very brief, including his act of zealousness. However, as is the Torah's way, it says exactly what has to be learned, concisely, summing up his nation-saving act in the following way:

> Pinchas ben Elazar ben Aharon HaKohen saw and got up from within the assembly and took a spear in his hand. (*Bamidbar* 25:7)

Of the three aspects of what Pinchas did—he saw, he got up, and took a spear—the first is the most important, because everything else depended upon it:

> What did he see? Rav said: He saw what was happening and remembered the *halachah* ... Shmuel said: He saw that *"There is no wisdom nor understanding nor counsel against God"* (*Mishlei* 21:30): whenever the Divine Name is being profaned, honor must not be paid to one's teacher. Rav Yitzchak said in Rebi Elazar's name: He saw the angel wreaking destruction amongst the people. (*Sanhedrin* 82a)

Of the three million Jews who had heard the law of what to do when a Jew takes a non-Jewish woman in public, he was the only one who recalled what to do? Unlikely. Rather, "seeing" here means that he appreciated what he saw, and sprung into action. Everyone saw what was happening, but didn't make the connection between what was taking place, what to do about it, and what would happen if they didn't take the appropriate action. Pinchas did.

> It was taught in a *brisa*: Rebi Yosi taught, "Woe to the creations that see, but do not know what they see ... (*Chagigah* 12b)

Furthermore, it is a common reaction in the Torah community that, when it comes to the big issues, it is wiser to leave them for the "big people". *E m u n a s Chachamim*—faith in the wise men—says that the rabbis know more than we do, that they are better connected than we are, and are more rational when it comes to dealing with crises.

On top of all that, because they are the leaders of the Jewish people, they get more *siyita d'Shemaya* than we can ever hope to receive. How many stories have been told of *rabbanim* who decided the *halachah* correctly, in spite of the fact that, inadvertently, they were told the wrong information? More than likely, this was also what held back many would-be zealots from acting when Zimri took Kozbi before the eyes of the people.

After all, Moshe *Rabbeinu* had been there, the Sanhedrin had been there, and the princes had been there. They had all witnessed the terrible profanation of God's Name, so certainly, if anyone should have acted and put an end to the crisis, it should have been them.

That's why, explains the Midrash, after Pinchas had done the deed, they began to chide him (*Sanhedrin* 82b), and might have killed him, had God not intervened, setting the record straight, and telling us what it takes to be a true zealot, for any cause.

Sometimes being a zealot for God is so important, that even the little guy can get a chance to be the "redeemer" from a crisis.

Dedicated in memory of our beloved parents

Max and Ethel Florence
Cape Town, South Africa

They performed tremendous acts of kindness, especially with respect to *Eretz Yisroel*.

May their *neshamot* have an *aliyah* b'Gan Aiden.
Michelle Kahn & Michael Florence

Av 27

DAY FIFTY-THREE:
For God's Sake

After the plague was over, and the Jewish people were in a recovery mode, God told Moshe *Rabbeinu*:

> *"Pinchas, the son of Elazar, the son of Aharon HaKohen, stopped My anger towards the Children of Israel, because he was zealous on My behalf, which prevented Me from destroying them because of jealousy."* (*Bamidbar* 25:10-11)

God wasn't just praising Pinchas' act, He was telling everyone why Pinchas had succeeded against the odds, and why he had been able to take action at a time that even his teachers had not: he had acted completely on behalf of God, not on behalf of himself. If he had felt any personal feelings about what Zimri was doing, he had cast them aside, relating to the crisis from God's perspective, not his own.

This was not something that Pinchas had learned to do at the moment of the crisis, as the Midrash teaches:

> *"They were crying at the opening of the Appointed Tent"* (*Bamidbar* 25:6); their hands became weakened at that moment ... At the end of the 40 years, as the Jewish people camped by the Jordan river ready to cross over into *Eretz Yisroel* ... they went ahead and acted promiscuously, weakening

Moshe and the righteous people with him. *"They cried"*?! Did Moshe not stand up against 600,000, as it says, *"He took the calf which they had made"* (Shemos 32:20)? His hands were weakened?! Rather, [Moshe was made to forget the law] in order for Pinchas to take that which he deserved. (*Bamidbar Rabbah* 20:24)

Deserved? What did he do previously to deserve to be such a hero on behalf of the floundering nation? We only briefly find out about him in *Parashas VaAira* (*Shemos* 6:25), and then again at the end of *Parashas Balak*. Where does it tell us what made Pinchas unique?

In the verse itself, when it traces his lineage back to his grandfather, Aharon *HaKohen*. As we learn from Ya'akov *Avinu*, whenever the Torah traces a person's lineage back to his ancestor, it is to associate his actions with those for which the ancestor became well known (*Rashi, Bereishis* 49:6). And, if ever there was a zealot on behalf of God, it had been Aharon *HaKohen*, as the *Rambam* writes (*Yad Chazakah, Hilchos Talmud Torah*, 3:1).

Another example of this idea is the *Bnos Tzelofchad*, who had the merit of being the ones through whom a *halachah* regarding inheritance was introduced in the Torah:

> The daughters of Tzelofchad—the son of Cheifer, the son of Gilad, the son of Machir, the son of Menashe, from the family of Menashe, the son of Yosef ... (*Bamidbar* 27:1)

> Why did it have to mention this, since it already says "the son of Menashe"? To tell you that Yosef loved the land, as it says, *"Bring my bones up"* (*Bereishis* 50:25), and that his "daughters" also loved the land, as it says, *"Give us our possession"* (*Bamidbar* 27:4). (*Rashi*)

In each case, it was not that the *Gadol HaDor* lacked or lost the merit to provide the direction at the critical moment in history. Rather, it was that someone else, because of his love of the *mitzvah*, merited to be the instrument of God at that moment in time. In fact, in each case, Moshe *Rabbeinu* was "held back" by Heaven to "make room" for the zealot to do his thing, with, as the Talmud explains, his blessing (*Sanhedrin* 82a), something that is not even necessary when *Chillul Hashem* is involved.

Today, unfortunately, that is almost always the case, whether we are talking about 80 percent assimilation, 52 percent intermarriage, or, as the prophet said, Jews spread throughout the world with little or no desire to return home. Not to mention a whole list of other issues and crises that *Klal Yisroel* is grappling with today.

So, you can take your pick; just don't avoid getting involved. For, as Mordechai told Esther:

> *"Do not imagine that you will be able to escape in the king's palace any more than the rest of the Jews. For if you continue to remain silent at a time like this, relief and salvation will come to the Jews from another place, while you and your father's house will perish. And who knows whether it was for such a time as this that you attained the royal position!"* (Esther 4:13)

Or, whatever position of influence we may have achieved in our own worlds.

Dedicated with the sincere hope that this book will inspire our fellow Jews to come home to Israel!

Anonymous

Av 28

DAY FIFTY-FOUR:
Heaven's Eye View

One of the more complicated issues to deal with, for a Torah Jew, is, "When does *hishtadalus*—personal effort—interfere with *bitachon*—trust in God?" On one hand, the *gemora* warns us not to rely upon miracles, either because the miracle won't happen for us, or even if it does, it won't come for free, but out of the reward we are destined to enjoy in the World-to-Come (*Shabbos* 32a).

On the other hand, the *gemora*, teaches:

> All is in the hands of Heaven except for fear Heaven. (*Brochos* 33b)

This means that, no matter what kind of effort we make in just about every area of life, the results are beyond our control, except for one: fear of God. Heaven leaves success in that area of life up to us.

It does not mean that Heaven does not help out with our developing fear of God; it certainly does. As the Talmud states:

> Anyone who comes to purify himself, they help him. (*Shabbos* 104a).

There can be no greater act of purification than striving to increase one's fear of God.

However, it is important to realize that there are two types of fear of God, as the *Ramchal* points out in *Mesillas Yesharim*. The most common is not fear of God Himself, but the fear of punishment that He may inflict upon us for committing a sin. On such a level, if a person thinks God doesn't see him committing the sin, or doesn't relate to the fact that God is watching him, even if it seems as if He isn't, he will commit the crime.

The second level of fear of God is far more sophisticated, and truer to the words, "*yiras Hashem*". For, the word "*yiras*" can mean, "the seeing of," as in "the seeing of God." However, not so much as in our seeing of God, which, of course, is not possible, but the seeing of God, that is, how God sees, specifically how He views the world and history.

There are two ways to view reality, God's way, and that of man's. God, being omnipotent and omniscient, knows everything; there is nothing He can't know. His perception of reality is 100 percent accurate, always was, and always will be. There is no such thing as misperception or misconception with respect to God.

This is not the case with respect to man. Man, though he often thinks he knows enough to correctly evaluate reality and the opportunity of the moment, usually doesn't. When you consider how many times men have misunderstood history and its needs, it is a wonder that we are still here. Actually, it is a miracle.

The goal of any human being, if he or she is going to fulfill his or her potential, must be to be able to perceive reality as accurately as possible. We must try to bring our perception of reality in line with God's, so that we can look at history through His eyes, so-to-speak. We must develop a Heaven's-eye view of life; that is true *yiras Shamayim*.

We are very pleased to be part of this important project, and to help bring its message to Jews who might not be aware of it yet, and to strengthen those who may already know it.

We hope that our involvement will be a merit for our family, wherever they may live, to help us all be a part of the *geulah b'rachamim*.

The Ray Family

Av 29

DAY FIFTY-FIVE:
Finding *Chayn*

Based upon the previous lesson, we can better understand a short, but highly instructive verse in the Torah:

> Noach found chayn —grace—in the eyes of God. (*Bereishis* 6:8)

This verse tells us Noach why survived the Flood, even though, by Noach's time, God had "regretted" making Creation. Though everyone else in the world angered God by their immoral behavior, God found something in Noach that He liked, something important enough to justify his miraculous survival from the tumultuous waters of the Great Flood.

However, if the verse is taken literally, it can actually tell us what was unique about Noach: he found grace in the eyes of God. In other words, when Noach looked into the "eyes" of God, he found something called "*chayn*", which happens to spell "Noach" in reverse: *Ches-Nun—Nun-Ches*. This is what you would expect to see if you held the letters up in front of someone's eyes, which reflect imagines like a mirror does.

This is all quite conceptual because, after all, God does not have eyes that we can look into. So, then, what does all of this mean? Well, what do eyes really represent, if not the vision of reality of a person. As much as seeing requires the receiving of light, the main function of the eyes is to allow us to look out at the world, and our analysis of what we see, and how we relate to it, is called our "out-look".

Therefore, what the verse is really telling us is that Noach was saved because he looked at the world through God's eyes. Noach, unlike the rest of his generation, saw reality as God saw it, and that is why he lived his life differently than anyone else. He found *chayn*.

For, *chayn* is much more than grace. It is what emanates from a person when he acts God-like. It is the light of the soul that is sensed by others from a person who allows his soul to guide his actions. This is why the trait of *chayn* is associated with Yosef:

> A son of chayn is Yosef. (*Rashi, Bereishis 49:22*)

regarding whom it says:

> God was with Yosef, and he became a successful man ... His master perceived that God was with him, and whatever he did God made succeed in his hand. (*Bereishis 39:2-3*)

> Pharaoh said to his servants, "Could we find another like him—a man in whom is the spirit of God?" (*Bereishis 41:37-38*)

Hence, the *gemora* concludes:

> Whoever has chayn has fear of God. (*Succah 49b*)

This is because, such a person sees reality as God does, which allows to see past the illusionary façade of the everyday physical world, past the "body" of Creation and into its soul. It is this knowledge that makes *mitzvos* meaningful, and what makes sin futile and wasteful.

It was this knowledge that gave Noach the courage to stand apart from the society around him, and make him brave enough to pursue a Godly lifestyle in a Godless world. It was this knowledge, ultimately, that saved him from catastrophe.

Thousands of years later, the knowledge is even more pertinent than ever, and the need to see past the façade of the materialistic world, just as crucial.

Av 30

DAY FIFTY-SIX:
Eyes of A Dove

He waited another seven days and again sent the dove from the ark. The dove came to him in the evening and behold, there was an olive leaf torn off in her mouth. (Bereishit 8:11)

Torn off : The Midrash explains this to mean food, and interprets "in her mouth" as speaking, i.e., she said, "Rather that my food be bitter as an olive but from the hand of God, than as sweet as honey from the hand of mortal men." (*Rashi*)

In other words, the dove told Noach, "*Nothing is better than living with the knowledge that God is the hand that feeds you, even if it means eating bitter food.*" The dove's message is not that man should forsake physical pleasure in this world; there is plenty to enjoy in life without even coming close to violating one's relationship with God.

Rather, the dove's message to Noach was, "*Don't forget what led to the downfall of mankind and brought about the Flood! It was man's insatiable need for physical pleasure, as if such pleasure was a goal unto itself. The goal of Creation is to be close to God, to be like Him, even if it means sacrificing physical comfort and pleasure to do so. Remember this,*" the dove reminded Noach, "*and mankind will avoid sliding to such physical destruction again.*"

Lest we mistakenly think that such danger only exists

for those who do not live by Torah, the *Ramban* explains otherwise:

> God told Moshe, "Speak to the entire congregation of the Children of Israel and tell them, 'Be holy, for I, your God, am holy.'" (*Vayikra* 19:1-2)

> BE HOLY: In my opinion, this "separation" is not from forbidden relationships, as he (i.e., *Rashi*) says, but it is the kind of separation mentioned throughout Torah when it comes to being elevated. For, the Torah warned us regarding forbidden relationships and forbidden foods, but it also permitted spousal intimacy and [kosher] meat and wine. Thus, a person with strong physical desires could behave immodestly with his own wife ... and eat [kosher] meat and drink wine in a disgusting manner, since the Torah has not yet forbidden this. Nevertheless, [if he acted in this manner] he would be a "*menuval b'reshus HaTorah*"—"disgusting with that which the Torah permits." Therefore, after the Torah specified what is certainly forbidden, it returned to tell us that we should exercise restraint with that which is permissible. (*Ramban*, *Vayikra* 19:2)

The physical world exists as a means to become closer to God, which means using it in a Godly manner. If so, then its value is derived by its ability to facilitate a closer relationship with God, not by how physically pleasurable it is. When the latter becomes the priority, warned the *yonah*, the animal to which the Jewish people are compared (*Brochos* 53b), we tend to lose sight of the purpose of life, the goal of Torah.

Or, even worse, *God forbid*, we cease to justify our success and existence, as Jewish history has shown time-and-time again.

Elul 1

DAY FIFTY-SEVEN:
A Different Type of Yonah

On Yom Kippur, the holiest day of the year, we read about a different type of *yonah*. During *Minchah* that day, we read *Maftir Yonah*, a very coveted honor for which many often bid significant sums of money to receive.

There are various explanations as to why we read about this specific prophet on such a spiritual day. However, none of them seem to point out one very important point of the story, which may be one of the most important lessons of life for a Jew.

Yonah had been summoned by God to warn the people of Nineveh that, unless they did *teshuvah*, their great city would be overturned. Yonah, suspecting that they would heed the warning, and therefore, they would not be destroyed, worried about looking like a false prophet, and, about making his own people look bad. Unlike the people of Nineveh, the Jewish people of that time did not heed the prophets' adjurations to do *teshuvah* before it was too late.

As a result, Yonah fled both his cherished homeland and the responsibility of the prophecy with which he had been entrusted. As he ran away, he boarded a ship that set sail for Tarshish, without his fellow sailors knowing who he was and what he was trying to do.

However, it did not take long before God whipped up

a mighty storm that threatened to sink the ship in which Yonah had taken refuge. As a result, everyone else on board panicked and immediately did whatever they could to appease whatever god might be responsible for the raging storm.

When all else failed, they realized that Yonah was missing, and went looking for him. To their utter shock, they found him sleeping, and soundly yet, in the hold of the ship, in spite of the angry movements of the ship. How could a person sleep through such a storm, and so peacefully yet?

They woke him up, and explained the predicament. He explained who he was, and that the storm, no doubt, was because of him. They implored him to pray to God to end the storm, but he told them that nothing short of throwing him overboard would save them and their ship, and very reluctantly, they complied, and the storm subsided. The rest is history in the book itself.

The fact that the Jewish people are compared to a *yonah* means that the story has additional layers of meaning that apply to the nation as a whole. Indeed, it may be a warning of a certain nature within the Jewish people that prevents us from acknowledging the storm taking place around us, until it is too late. Even though the gentiles all around us panic about current predicaments, we have often just looked the other way as the storm clouds gather all around us.

The moral of the story is, when God talks to you, listen. And, if He tells you things, pay attention to what He says. This means being sensitive to the events of your life, especially the unusual ones, and trying to understand what they might mean in terms if your direction in life.

Most important of all, if He gives you the opportunity to make a difference, don't run in the opposite direction. Above all, don't "sleep" in the "hold" while the sea rages around you. That is, don't focus only on your own life and personal issues while the world around you is in crisis, and while the rest of the people run around frantically to save the day!

Elul 2

DAY FIFTY-EIGHT:
Listen to the Message

"But," you may ask, *"who hears God speak today? The Era of Prophecy ended thousands of years ago. Anyone who claims to hear God speak today probably has psychological problems and may be dangerous!"*

True, but God has many ways of getting His message across to His people. Even at this late stage of history, when even *Ruach HaKodesh* may be a rarity, God talks to His people, at least those willing to hear what He has to say. It's what we refer to as *Hashgochah Pratis*—Divine Providence.

Everything in history is a function of *Hashgochah Pratis*, as the *gemora* states:

> Rebi Chanina said: A person does not damage his finger below unless they declare it above, as it says, *"By God are a strong man's footsteps established"* (*Tehillim* 37:23). (*Chullin* 7b)

> There isn't a blade of grass below that does not have a *mazel* in Heaven hitting it, telling it, "Grow!" (*Bereishis Rabbah* 10:6)

It may not always be clear how or why something happens, but by definition, it is always a function of the will of God. To believe otherwise is to take power away from God and give it to something else, which is the classic definition of idol worship. Thus, the *gemora* teaches that a Jew must believe:

> *Ain od Milvado*—then is no other being controlling the events of this world but God Himself. (Sanhedrin 66b)

The question is, how does one know if the events of his time are unique in as much as they are a direct message from Heaven about the direction of history? Just as it is easy to make nothing of something, it is easy to make something of nothing, as so many false messiahs have done in the past. Before a person invests himself and risks his credibility for the rest of his life, he needs to know that the messages about the events of history are, in fact, real messages.

Dovid *HaMelech* answered this question. Perhaps, anticipating future times when the Jewish people would need prophecy to guide them, but would lack the prophets to provide it, he composed the words:

> *This is from God, that which is wondrous in our eyes. (Tehillim 118:23)*

But, isn't everything from God? Of course it is. If so, then what insight did Dovid *HaMelech* provide future generations with this verse? A way to translate the events of our times into messages from Heaven, and if necessary, warnings as well.

Essentially, the ancestor of *Moshiach* was saying that, if something happens in history that catches us by surprise, or in a way that seems to be the opposite of what we would or should expect, then it can be seen as act of direct Divine Providence.

If some event, or series of events, is wondrous to us, instructed Dovid *HaMelech*, then it can be considered to be a sign from Heaven of the current direction of history, and knowing this, it seems, is the first step to being able to take note of such events, and understand their meaning. Such spiritual sensitivity is what has always allowed certain individuals throughout Jewish history to make a difference, and, on many occasions, a *big* difference.

Elul 3

DAY FIFTY-NINE:
Merit To Be Redeemed

The Midrash records a remarkable exchange that is so important for understanding the mechanics of redemption, and yet, it is barely known. It says:

> When Moshe came and told the Jewish people that, in this month, you will be redeemed they told him, "Moshe *Rabbe-inu*, how can we be redeemed? All of Egypt is sullied from our idol worship!" He answered them, "Since He wants you to be redeemed, He does not look at your idol worship but instead, He *'skips over mountains'* (*Shir HaShirim* 2:8)" (*Shir HaShirim Rabbah* 2:8:2) ... This is because all redemptions are the result of a revelation of *Arich Anpin*. He explained to the Jewish people that, The Holy One, Blessed is He, was dealing with them on the level of the light of *Arich Anpin* called "*Ayin*", which works above any measure. In other words, it does not depend upon merit or demerit. (*Sha'arei Leshem*, p. 113)

Thus, when it comes to a *keitz*, that is, a pre-designated time for redemption on any level, God employs a special light that does not flow because of our merits, or stop flowing because of our sins. Rather, it flows regardless, performing its miracles only because the time has come for redemption, according to the Divine plan.

That was true for the redemption from Egypt, and it will be true for the Final Redemption as well:

> Furthermore, they are destined to be redeemed in the future as well in *Yemos HaMoshiach*, and the light then will also not be the result of merit or good deeds at all, as it says, *"You have sold yourselves for nothing, and you shall be redeemed without money"* (Yeshayahu 52:3). That is, without *teshuvah* or good deeds. (Ibid.)

This is a remarkable concept, especially as we look at the Jewish world today. Eighty percent assimilation rate. Over 50 percent of Jews marrying today do so outside of their faith. Not a good situation at all, and one that is tremendous reason for concern, since Heaven does not tolerate such situations forever. Once again, the question becomes, "How can we be redeemed when all of 'Egypt' is sullied from our idol worship!"

The answer is, simply, because the time has come. Once a *keitz* arrives, the only thing that concerns God is redeeming every last Jew alive, regardless of his previous record. After all, people like Dasan and Aviram left with Moshe *Rabbeinu* and the rest of the nation, not to mention Michah, who took his idol along with him.

Thus, the four-fifths in Egypt should have survived the Plague of Darkness, since redemption did not require merit, and sin did not disqualify someone from leaving. However, you can't redeem someone who doesn't want to leave exile, and that was the criteria that determined who left Egypt, and who stayed behind.

So, while it is absolutely crucial to constantly strengthen ourselves in Torah and *mitzvos,* and reach out to those who are distant from both, it is extremely crucial to be open to whatever redemption, and the lead-up to re-demption, means. How we feel about the *Geulah Shlaimah* today can determine our right to be redeemed tomorrow.

Elul 4

DAY SIXTY:
Geulah b'Rachamim

To date, the Jewish people are 3,319 years old. At least, that is how long we have had Torah for, having received it 2448 years from Creation, in the year 1313 BCE. We became a nation while still in Egypt, but we became a Torah nation at Mt. Sinai after receiving the Torah directly from God.

And yet, the nation that stood at Mt. Sinai and said the words, *"We will do, and we will understand"* (*Shemos* 24:7), had only been a fraction of its former self, only 3,000,000 from a population that previously had numbered five times that amount. Four-fifths, 12,000,000 Jews died in the Plague of Darkness, as *Rashi* explains, because they had chosen to remain behind in Egypt (*Shemos* 10:22).

The Plague of Darkness was the only one of the 10 plagues inflicted on the Egyptian people that also affected the Jewish people. The question is, was it an isolated event, or does it have a message for the generations of Jews that survived, and followed?

It has been pointed out that there may be an allusion to the Holocaust in this very plague that resulted in the death of millions of Jews. In advance of the plague, God told Moshe:

"Stretch out your hand towards Heaven, so that darkness will come over Egypt, a darkness which can be felt." (*Shemos* 10:21)

In Hebrew, *"a darkness which will be felt"* is written, *"vayamish choshech"*, spelled: *Vav-Yud-Mem-Shin*—which will be felt—*Ches-Shin-Chof*—darkness. However, in the *Aleph-Bais*, the letter that precedes *Vav-Yud-Mem-Shin*, a valid form of *gematria*, is *Heh-Tes-Lamed-Raish*, which is how the word "Hitler" (*y"s*), would be transliterated.

Mere coincidence, or an amazing occurrence, considering that the Plague of Darkness was the only one to kill Jews, and millions yet?

Furthermore, as mentioned already, as Torah Jews, we do not believe in random occurrence, and especially in this case, since the *gemora* itself connects up the Final Redemption with the first one. It even warns that what went wrong in the first redemption may actually be repeated in the final one, *God forbid* (*Sanhedrin* 111a), making it somewhat difficult to ignore the implication of such a hint.

If something happens historically, it is sanctioned by Heaven. If we become aware of it, then that too was planned by God. This is especially true since God is always trying to communicate with us, and save us from disaster, whenever possible.

Thus, the *Ben Ish Chai* points out that even one of the terms used for the Final Redemption, *"Keitz HaYomim"*—end of days—alludes to the connection between the redemption at the beginning of history, and the one at the end of it. The *gematria* of *"keitz"*, spelled *Kuf-Tzaddi*, is 190. This was the amount of years remaining from the 400 years we were supposed to have spent in Egypt, but didn't, having left early after only 210 years.

Even the word "*hayomim*" is instructive. It would have been enough to say "*keitz yomim*" to say "end of days"; *keitz hayomim* means "end of the days," which might have been meaningless without the 190-year reference that precedes it. Which days end with *Yemos HaMoshiach*? "Those days," meaning the days left over from the Egyptian exile, revealing, as mentioned earlier (Lessons 19 and 20), that the Final Redemption is really just the conclusion of the first one.

This means, that the redemption from Egypt is a work in progress, and only comes to a conclusion with the advent of *Yemos HaMoshiach*. Not only are the two redemptions connected, but they are really two ends of one long, ongoing journey to freedom. More than the Jewish people have been waiting for the Final Redemption, history has been waiting for the Final Redemption, and that is the reason why it hasn't come to this very day.

The *Chofetz Chaim* compared the Final Redemption to the payment of a *sachir yom*—a daily worker. The law is that, if a person works on a daily basis, then he must be paid for his day's work at the day's end. To not do so is a violation of a Torah *mitzvah*, unless, explains the *Chofetz Chaim*, the worker does not request his payment.

Likewise, explained the *Chofetz Chaim*, God definitely owes us the Final Redemption, especially after all we have suffered to fulfill the Torah. But, he explains, if we don't ask for *geulah*, then God can put off bringing it until we finally demand it. And, it is always better to ask for something at a time that you don't need it, than to wait for the time that you do.

Over 3,000 years of Jewish history can testify to that.

Four-fifths of the Jewish population in Egypt did not merit to survive because they rejected the redemption at hand.

The Generation of the Spies suffered a similar fate because, not learning the lesson of the four-fifths, rejected *Eretz Yisroel*.

How many times has God built us up as a people, only to take it all away from us again? Why? Because all of our success has always only been to further the cause of redemption, and it is justified as long as this is the case. When it stops being the case, and it only serves to further the cause of exile, we usually lose just about all of it.

Once again, the Jewish people find themselves in a similar position. We have lived through another golden era, and even possess *Eretz Yisroel*, after 2,000 years of being away from the land. In the meantime, the winds of change suggest that a downturn might be heading our way once again.

Do we learn from our past mistakes, and finally take the right course of action, becoming *geulah*-oriented, and yearn for *Kibbutz Golios*, the return of the temple, and the *Shechinah* to *Tzion*? Or, do we continue to miss the point, and instead remain focused on secondary issues, blinded by confusing political matters?

This is the question that every Jew who can ask it must answer, and answering the former is crucial for bringing the Final Redemption, in mercy.

May it be so speedily in our time. *Amen*.

	Cycle 1	Cycle 2	Cycle 3	Cycle 4	Cycle 5	Cycle 6
1	Tamm. 4	Elul 5	Chesh. 6	Teves 7	Adar 8	Iyar 9
2	Tamm. 5	Elul 6	Chesh. 7	Teves 8	Adar 9	Iyar 10
3	Tamm. 6	Elul 7	Chesh. 8	Teves 9	Adar 10	Iyar 11
4	Tamm. 7	Elul 8	Chesh. 9	Teves 10	Adar 11	Iyar 12
5	Tamm. 8	Elul 9	Chesh. 10	Teves 11	Adar 12	Iyar 13
6	Tamm. 9	Elul 10	Chesh. 11	Teves 12	Adar 13	Iyar 14
7	Tamm. 10	Elul 11	Chesh. 12	Teves 13	Adar 14	Iyar 15
8	Tamm. 11	Elul 12	Chesh. 13	Teves 14	Adar 15	Iyar 16
9	Tamm. 12	Elul 13	Chesh. 14	Teves 15	Adar 16	Iyar 17
10	Tamm. 13	Elul 14	Chesh. 15	Teves 16	Adar 17	Iyar 18
11	Tamm. 14	Elul 15	Chesh. 16	Teves 17	Adar 18	Iyar 19
12	Tamm. 15	Elul 16	Chesh. 17	Teves 18	Adar 19	Iyar 20
13	Tamm. 16	Elul 17	Chesh. 18	Teves 19	Adar 20	Iyar 21
14	Tamm. 17	Elul 18	Chesh. 19	Teves 20	Adar 21	Iyar 22
15	Tamm. 18	Elul 19	Chesh. 20	Teves 21	Adar 22	Iyar 23
16	Tamm. 19	Elul 20	Chesh. 21	Teves 22	Adar 23	Iyar 24
17	Tamm. 20	Elul 21	Chesh. 22	Teves 23	Adar 24	Iyar 25
18	Tamm. 21	Elul 22	Chesh. 23	Teves 24	Adar 25	Iyar 26
19	Tamm. 22	Elul 23	Chesh. 24	Teves 25	Adar 26	Iyar 27
20	Tamm. 23	Elul 24	Chesh. 25	Teves 26	Adar 27	Iyar 28
21	Tamm. 24	Elul 25	Chesh. 26	Teves 27	Adar 28	Iyar 29
22	Tamm. 25	Elul 26	Chesh. 27	Teves 28	Adar 29	Sivan 1
23	Tamm. 26	Elul 27	Chesh. 28	Teves 29	Nissan 1	Sivan 2
24	Tamm. 27	Elul 28	Chesh. 29	Shevat 1	Nissan 2	Sivan 3
25	Tamm. 28	Elul 29	Kislev 1	Shevat 2	Nissan 3	Sivan 4
26	Tamm. 29	Tish. 1	Kislev 2	Shevat 3	Nissan 4	Sivan 5
27	Av 1	Tish. 2	Kislev 3	Shevat 4	Nissan 5	Sivan 6
28	Av 2	Tish. 3	Kislev 4	Shevat 5	Nissan 6	Sivan 7
29	Av 3	Tish. 4	Kislev 5	Shevat 6	Nissan 7	Sivan 8
30	Av 4	Tish. 5	Kislev 6	Shevat 7	Nissan 8	Sivan 9

31	Av 5	Tish. 6	Kislev 7	Shevat 8	Nissan 9	Sivan 10
32	Av 6	Tish. 7	Kislev 8	Shevat 9	Nissan 10	Sivan 11
33	Av 7	Tish. 8	Kislev 9	Shevat 10	Nissan 11	Sivan 12
34	Av 8	Tish. 9	Kislev 10	Shevat 11	Nissan 12	Sivan 13
35	Av 9	Tish. 10	Kislev 11	Shevat 12	Nissan 13	Sivan 14
36	Av 10	Tish. 11	Kislev 12	Shevat 13	Nissan 14	Sivan 15
37	Av 11	Tish. 12	Kislev 13	Shevat 14	Nissan 15	Sivan 16
38	Av 12	Tish. 13	Kislev 14	Shevat 15	Nissan 16	Sivan 17
39	Av 13	Tish. 14	Kislev 15	Shevat 16	Nissan 17	Sivan 18
40	Av 14	Tish. 15	Kislev 16	Shevat 17	Nissan 18	Sivan 19
41	Av 15	Tish. 16	Kislev 17	Shevat 18	Nissan 19	Sivan 20
42	Av 16	Tish. 17	Kislev 18	Shevat 19	Nissan 20	Sivan 21
43	Av 17	Tish. 18	Kislev 19	Shevat 20	Nissan 21	Sivan 22
44	Av 18	Tish. 19	Kislev 20	Shevat 21	Nissan 22	Sivan 23
45	Av 19	Tish. 20	Kislev 21	Shevat 22	Nissan 23	Sivan 24
46	Av 20	Tish. 21	Kislev 22	Shevat 23	Nissan 24	Sivan 25
47	Av 21	Tish. 22	Kislev 23	Shevat 24	Nissan 25	Sivan 26
48	Av 22	Tish. 23	Kislev 24	Shevat 25	Nissan 26	Sivan 27
49	Av 23	Tish. 24	Kislev 25	Shevat 26	Nissan 27	Sivan 28
50	Av 24	Tish. 25	Kislev 26	Shevat 27	Nissan 28	Sivan 28
51	Av 25	Tish. 26	Kislev 27	Shevat 28	Nissan 29	Sivan 29
52	Av 26	Tish. 27	Kislev 28	Shevat 29	Nissan 30	Sivan 29
53	Av 27	Tish. 28	Kislev 29	Shevat 30	Iyar 1	Sivan 30
54	Av 28	Tish. 29	Kislev 30	Adar 1	Iyar 2	Sivan 30
55	Av 29	Tish. 30	Teves 1	Adar 2	Iyar 3	Tamm. 1
56	Av 30	Chesh. 1	Teves 2	Adar 3	Iyar 4	Tamm. 1
57	Elul 1	Chesh. 2	Teves 3	Adar 4	Iyar 5	Tamm. 2
58	Elul 2	Chesh. 3	Teves 4	Adar 5	Iyar 6	Tamm. 2
59	Elul 3	Chesh. 4	Teves 5	Adar 6	Iyar 7	Tamm. 3
60	Elul 4	Chesh. 5	Teves 6	Adar 7	Iyar 8	Tamm. 3

SOURCES

If they humble their hearts, if they accept the punishment for their wrongdoings, then will I remember My covenant with Ya'akov, My covenant with Yitzchak, and My covenant with Avraham. I will remember the land, which will have been left behind by them, enjoying its rests, lying desolate without them.
(Vayikra 26:41-42)

Everything in life is a matter of *Hashgochah Pratis* —Divine Providence—because, everything is a functional of the will of God. It's just that, most of the time, Heavenly help comes in ways that can give people the wrong impression that Heaven is not involved in their affairs, what we call *b'derech teva*—through natural means. This is because the name of the game is free-will, and free-will means choosing good because it is right, not because it is obvious.

However, sometimes, Heavenly help is so obvious that you get the feeling that God is right there with you, encouraging you along your way. How many times has information showed up just at the right time, in just the right way, against the odds?

Sometimes, *Hashgochah Pratis* works in the opposite manner as well. Sometimes, information that we think ought to have been known for the longest time, because of its importance, has remained hidden, or known to only a few fortunate people. Seemingly, sometimes, God holds back information, either because we don't merit to know it, or because the time is not yet right to reveal it.

One such important piece of information is a letter that is said to have come from the Abarbanel (1437-1508). Before two weeks ago, I had never heard of the letter, in spite of the fact that I have been learning Jewish history for years, and especially from an exile-redemption point-of-view. I had never even seen a reference to it.

This is what the letter says:

"And now I will reveal to you something, and it is something that was received from the mouths of the prophets. In the final days, after which there will be no more, the most awesome war, since Creation, will occur in the world. In a city in a western country, an evil person will arise and rule with anger and fury, and he will command the total destruction of the Jewish nation. The Jewish people will be in great trouble, and he will rule for seven years, as it says in the prophets. He will go out to war to conquer the entire world, and all the nations of the world will gather; not one will be missing … On one side will stand the nations that believe, and on the other side will stand the nations that don't believe, and the evil one will overcome each people under his foot, nation after nation. All the kings of the east and west will be overcome by him, and they will fall before him like garlic peels. He will have no mercy on them, and he will trample them like a lion. His kingdom will spread to almost the entire world. Some he will conquer without any bloodshed, and some he will completely destroy. It was about this that Bilaam spoke prophetically when he said, '*Oh! Who will survive when he imposes these—mesumo el —Aleph-Lamed!*' (*Bamidbar* 24:23): when this evil person will arise in the world, his name and the name of his mother will be alluded to by the letters *Aleph-Lamed*. The side of holiness will join together with the Other Side. This is the War of Gog and Magog, and he will be victorious until he comes to the holy land of the Jewish people. Then, the righteous shoot of our redemption will sprout ..."

It is a remarkable letter that seems to have predicted the Holocaust, 500 years in advance, and the return to *Eretz Yisroel* of the Jewish people as a result. The Chofetz Chaim certainly saw the future World War II as a War of Gog and Magog, and everyone knows about the miraculous turn of events, in the Battle of El Alamein, that stopped Rommel from entering *Eretz Yisroel* and destroying the defenseless communities that lived there.

However, if this letter is in fact talking about World War II and the Holocaust, it would make what has happened since then, in *Eretz Yisroel,* part of the Final Redemption process. This would certainly explain the miraculous record of survival of the Jews living on the land, and the incredible growth that has taken place there over the last 60 years.

It certainly validates the idea that we are living in very special times. Special times, with special needs, and only by meeting those needs can we usher in the Final Redemption, peacefully.

For more information regarding Rabbi Pinchas Winston, any of his projects, or to purchase something from the Thirtysix.org online bookstore, go to:

www.thirtysix.org.